COLLINS GEM
CATS

COLLINS GEM
AS

C000097284

COLLINS GEM
HORSES
& PONIES
a mine of information

COLLINS GEM
INSECTS
a mine of information

COLLINS GEM
**KINGS &
QUEENS**
a mine of information

MUSHROOMS
& TOADSTOOLS
a mine of information

COLLINS GEM
SNAKES
a mine of information

COLLINS GEM
SPIDERS
a mine of information

COLLINS GEM
STRESS
Survival Guide
a mine of information

COLLINS GEM
TAROT
a mine of information

COLLINS GEM
WINE
Guide
a mine of information

COLLINS GEM
WORLD
atlas
a mine of information

COLLINS GEM
YOGA
a mine of information

COLLINS GEM
ZODIAC
Types
a mine of information

COLLINS GEM

BEER

Ronald Atkins

HarperCollins*Publishers*

HarperCollins Publishers
PO Box, Glasgow G4 0NB

First published 1997
This edition published 1999

Reprint 10 9 8 7 6 5 4 3 2

ISBN 0 00 472261-2

Printed in Italy by Amadeus S.p.A.

CONTENTS

ACKNOWLEDGEMENTS

I would like to thank all the various breweries and trade organisations who have helped in the assembly of material for use in this book.

In particular, for all kinds of help, my thanks go to: Trevor Havard (Beeston Maltings), Paul Corbett (Charles Faram Hops), Miles Jenner (Harvey's Brewery), Tim Hampson and Jan Booth (British Licensed Retailers Association), Phil Johnson (Beer Direct), Michael Cook (Premier Beers), Chris Marchbanks, Keith Thomas (Brewlab), Michael Hardman, John Nancollis, Iain Loe (CAMRA), and Peter Crombecq (EBCU).

Ronald Atkins
London, 1997

A BRIEF HISTORY OF BEER

There's no mention of it in the Book of Genesis, but beer does go back a very, very long way. Our distant ancestors discovered how to grow barley and make primitive versions of bread and cakes. Juice from damp barley, left uncovered and therefore likely to pick up wild yeast floating in the air the way Belgium's lambic beers are brewed to this day, became one of the first alcoholic beverages. Beer brewing seems to have begun in the Middle East by 3000 BC at the latest, in the terrain between the modern cities of Baghdad and Basra (Mesopotamia, Babylon and Sumer).

Something resembling the modern brewing industry soon emerged. Haphazard wetting and drying was replaced by germinating the barley in earthenware pots and/or 'kilning' it by the fire and then using it, as malt is today, in all kinds of culinary activities, not just to make beer. As a protection against swallowing specks of yeast and other floating matter, the Egyptians usually drank their beer through a reed, an early version of the modern straw. The Egyptians also brewed with malted wheat: a recently excavated kitchen in the Sun Temple of Queen Nefertiti included a brewery whose contents were analysed and, eventually, reproduced by Scottish-Courage as a mash of malted emmer – the brand of wheat found in the old brewhouse – and

9

flavoured with juniper and coriander, two of the spices grown in Egypt that would have been added to counteract the malt flavour. Some years earlier, the Anchor brewery in San Francisco had based a beer on Babylonian practice, using bread laced with honey in the mash and then boiling it with dates.

From Egypt, the secret of making beer spread around the known world. The Greeks provide possibly the first instances of wine-snobbery, relegating beer as the drink for those at the lower end of the social ladder. Ancient Romans did much the same, but they recognized the value of beer, perhaps discovered in the lands they took over, by giving it to their all-conquering soldiers (these were said to march on beer and vinegar). By the time they reached England and Wales, the Romans knew enough about beer to be unimpressed by the local versions, and may have encouraged a more modern approach to malting and brewing.

Climatic conditions determine what food and drink a country produces. Northern Europe, whose moderate temperatures and substantial rainfall are not conducive to growing grapes, suited the growing of barley, whereas in the hotter, but non-wine-producing countries of South-East Asia, beer would be brewed with a substantial amount of rice. Brewing beer involves more complex processes than wine-making and this encouraged the development of a technology that involved the systematic skimming of yeast from one brew and adding it to the next, converting barley into different types of malt (by wetting and then kilning it) and manufacturing special vessels to heat and boil the mixture (known as 'wort', from the Old English wyrt) and then let the result ferment. The British may have introduced wooden casks, in which they stored mead and cider, to the beer industry. The word 'ale', soon adapted by most of the brewing countries, derives from the Danish word for oil, which is what the Vikings called their drink. The origin of the word 'beer' itself can be found in the Old English beor and the German bier, among others.

A traditional cooperage

Remember that the quality of water, which we take for granted today, was very unreliable until quite recent times. Boiling it to kill the dangerous impurities seemed a good idea. Additionally, the health-giving properties of malt had already been identified, and beer was seen as being rich in essential nutriments. Various deities and saints promoted beer: the Greek historian Heroditus claimed that Osiris was regarded as the Egyptians' god of beer, and even taught them to brew.

Such sponsorship is better documented in the case of St Arnold, regarded in Belgium as the patron saint of beer. Along with what we would nowadays call 'brewpubs', the most prolific breweries of the Middle Ages were the monasteries of Northern Europe. There were two overriding reasons to drink beer, both underlined by St Arnold: the dangers of untreated water, and the benefits of the vitamins the beer contained, regarded as essential dietary supplements for all, but especially for monks who otherwise led frugal lives and ate comparatively little (the corpulent, 'Friar Tuck' image did not apply to those spending most of their time in retreat).

The widespread belief that beer was good for you made it, along with bread, the staple part of many an adult's diet. Money could be made from it, not least by the authorities. In Britain, beer began to be taxed regularly during the reign of Henry II. These were mainly local taxes, but a national levy, a 'tax on

AT LUNCH

we all agree that

beer is best

MALT · HOPS · SUGAR · YEAST

moveables' that included beer, was raised in 1188 to help pay for the Crusades. This was repeated in 1228 and 1488.

Improved communications, both within countries and between them, gave enormous impetus to the commercial breweries, which could expand their horizons well beyond the towns or villages where

**Shire horses drawing beer
wagons were once a common site**

they were based. Beers marketed in this way would become what today we call 'brand names' with identifiable characteristics, the most celebrated early example being India Pale Ale, brewed at Burton upon Trent in central England and shipped across the ocean to help sustain the British troops fighting in India. The success of such brands encouraged emulation, and chemists would find ways to replicate the properties of the Burton water in IPAs brewed anywhere in the world.

The practice of flavouring beer with herbs, berries or spices was well established, but hops, now associated so closely with brewing, were a comparatively recent addition to the basic recipe, although some beers from Babylonian times onwards included them. Possibly first used regularly in modern times by the Germans, but soon spreading to Belgium and Holland, hops gave a distinctive taste but also – and this was crucial – helped to protect it against infection for longer periods. The dominant spicing and bittering agents by the 16th century, hops had to surmount a strong rearguard action fought by traditionalists, who no doubt proclaimed the virtues of the bog myrtle with the unrelenting zeal they would unleash today in defence of the hop.

This new sensation was referred to as 'beer' and unhopped beer was known as 'ale'. Today, this distinction has become blurred and in the following pages, 'ale' refers to beer fermented with yeast that traditionally rises to the top of the vessel, whereas 'lager' means beer produced by bottom-fermenting yeasts.

Unlike the hop plant, yeast has always been crucial to beer, even if no one understood exactly what it was and how it worked. From early times, brewers learnt how to skim yeast off one brew so it could be used in the next. Later, the Germans began fermenting beer at low temperatures underground: this took much longer, but the advantage was that the yeast stayed in pure condition because there nothing flying through the cold air to infect it. The beer was stored in a Lager (the German word for 'store') for up to six months before being drunk, from which emerged the English term, 'lager', as applied to certain beers. Since then, and especially after Louis Pasteur finally identified what yeast did and E.C. Hansen laid down how it should be treated, the hygienic control of yeast has been paramount in almost every kind of brewing.

That was a hundred years ago. Despite innumerable technical developments and refinements since, the brewing process has remained much the same. Malt, hops, yeast and water remain the essential components. To these can be added wheat, herbs, berries, fruits, honey and other ingredients that may have a long history in a particular country or a particular brew or may have just been dreamt up by the brewer as a means of imparting variety or to steal a march on the rest of the market.

HOW BEER IS BREWED

1. Ingredients

Water

Most beers consists of over 90% of water. In the old days, brewers would just collect water (always called 'liquor' in the trade) locally and make a brew. As certain beers became more widely available through commercial deals and improved transport, their inherent qualities inspired emulation. In the case of the Burton pale ales, the local water is naturally hardened by its heavy mineral content and includes gypsum, which is seen as an important ingredient: breweries producing pale ales a long way from Burton might get their boffins to add the appropriate salts to whatever liquor they used, and to remove any that were unwanted.

With top-fermented pale ales, hard water is usually considered an asset. On the other hand, pale lagers in the pilsener tradition use soft water. This also suits the darker ales, such as porter and stout.

Jennings draught bitter from England and Palm Speciale from Belgium have more colour than most so-called pale ales, and both use the soft water relatively untreated.

Before the technology to treat water could be relied upon, breweries tended to be sited near a spring, whose water was less likely to be polluted. Some still use their own spring water, though most recent arrivals take the local commercial product, which they can adjust as necessary.

Malt

From the beginning, malted barley has been a staple ingredient of beer. By medieval times, the techniques of steeping the barley in water to germinate the seed and turn starch into sugar, then applying heat by kilning it, had already become established. The processes have since been mechanized, automated and computerized, but the principles remain much the same.

After harvesting, the barley is bought by the malsters, who can keep it stored under slightly damp conditions for about two years, moisture being essential to stop the barley from deteriorating. Barley for malting is steeped in large vats and brought up to 44% moisture in controlled stages: steeping is interrupted from time to time, the water drained and the carbon dioxide gas given off replaced by air, which allows the grain to breathe and start producing enzymes.

In traditional floor maltings, the malt is then tipped on to the floor and moisture and temperature are again tightly controlled, while the seed germinates and continues to grow the embryo that will eventually convert to sugar when the beer is mashed. The final stage is the kilning that preserves the embryo in the state required for this conversion. Heat from the kiln dries the malt down to 2.5% moisture and cures it to provide the flavour brewers look for.

Turning the malt by hand

That describes how pale malt, by far the largest part of the mash in most beers, is produced. Such specialities as black, chocolate, crystal and amber malts may be added. Crystal malt imparts colour to bitters. Instead of being kilned, it is transferred in relatively small amounts to a roasting vessel in which the heat steadily increases while the starch converts to sugar. At the precise moment a clear, sugary liquid is obtained, the maltster cuts off the heat and douses the malt with water in order to preserve it in that state. Malts used in darker beers are kilned in the usual way, and then roasted to the required degree of colour and flavour.

The techniques of ale brewing in Britain were based on malt that is fully modified and has low nitrogen content, thus preventing unwanted haze in the finished product. Throughout much of mainland Europe, the barley, grown in a sunnier climate, was higher in nitrogen, so the malt tended to require more complex procedures at the brewery to reach the same result. This influenced the techniques developed for mashing lager, which from start to finish took much longer at lower temperatures, and needed malt with a higher nitrogen content to produce enzymic activity throughout this period.

Today, the big high-tech brewers of ale simply obtain whatever malt meets their price and let their machines and accumulated expertise do the rest. By contrast, many of the new small brewers have discovered the advantages of paying a bit more for high-quality malt that is simpler to work with.

Hops

Hops are by far the most recent addition to the list of essential ingredients. They were certainly used by brewers in Northern Europe during the 14th century, when it would have been noted widely that hopped beer tended to

21

keep longest and best of all. Before hops became universal, beer would have been spiced by various plants and herbs, depending on what was grown in the area or was otherwise available locally.

The preservative qualities of hops remain paramount in the making of some Belgian beers, notably the unique lambic, and they are still needed widely as a disinfectant. Lambics apart, however, hops today are chosen primarily for their flavours. Brewers rate hop plants according to their alpha acid content and divide them very broadly into 'bittering hops' and 'aroma hops': hops with a level of 8% or higher are generally used only for bitterness while those below this level may combine bittering qualities with less definable aromas. Such rigid distinctions are continually being bent, as brewers experiment by boiling with just one variety of hop instead of trying to blend flavours and by making ales with hops associated with lager, and vice versa. Bitterness levels, as measured in units, depend as much on the quantity used as on the intrinsic quality of the individual hop, while some well-hopped beers are not especially bitter.

Another traditional function of the hop flower was to act as a filter. At the end of the copper boil, the wort passes through a bed of spent hops that filters out floating particles (including stray bits of hop) as it passes through to be cooled and fermented. More modern systems of filtration by centrifuge (a whirlpool that traps the particles after the boil) have encouraged the use of hop pellets - compressed hops that some brewers prefer to use. Oil concentrates made from hops became a cheaper substitute for the real thing, but the resultant harshness has convinced some brewers either to stop using them in the boil or to reduce their role.

Yeast

Perhaps the most vital ingredient of the brew, yeast has the lowest public profile. Visitors on organized trips to breweries may be encouraged to chew grains of malt and to extract the flavours from whole hops by rubbing them with their hands. In most cases, though, the yeast used by the brewers will be kept wherever they have isolated it, to reduce the chance of it being infected.

The scientific control of ingredients is of paramount importance to brewers

The first yeasts to ferment beer wafted in the air. Those used today in the brewery will be hygienically controlled, brought out only when the wort has been boiled and cooled. Yeast is then added to provide two essential attributes – alcohol and carbon dioxide – without which beer would not be beer. Highly volatile, it reproduces itself and is cared for lovingly by many breweries, who for safety also stock samples in a central yeast bank. They realize that having to use a different yeast would alter the taste of well-established beers.

It has traditionally been divided into ale yeast, which rises to the surface of the vessel when fermenting the beer, and lager yeast that sinks to the bottom. Recent innovations include the use of traditional top-fermenting yeasts in sealed conical fermenters (the type once reserved exclusively for lagers) to produce ales. The outcome is a procedural compromise: most of the yeast sinks to the bottom and, though the fermentation time remains about the same, the ale is generally left to condition for longer than usual until racked.

Others

Such terms as 'adjuncts' and 'additives' have often been uttered with disdain. The German purity law, known as the *reinheitsgebot*, stipulates that beer should be brewed only with water, malt, hops and yeast, and there are brewers all over the world who follow this precept. Purists once frowned on any deviation that did not reflect long-standing practice – although one cannot, obviously, brew wheat beer without wheat – on the grounds the brewer was trying to cut corners or get away with spending less money. While that has been so in some cases, there are often more valid reasons. Some ingredients commonly used are listed below.

Torrefied wheat – wheat previously 'popped', rather like the puffed wheat found on breakfast tables, and then conditioned by heat and added to the mash, where it reacts with malt in a manner that improves the beer's ultimate ability to create and maintain a foaming head when served.

Flaked maize – dilutes the nitrogen produced by malt.

Malted wheat – malted in the same way as barley, wheat forms a significant part of the mash of German wheat beers.

Unmalted wheat – used in such Belgian specialities as Hoegaarden Witbier.

Rice – beers from the Far East, Central and South America and many produced by major brewers in the USA contain rice.; it is added to the mash after heat-conditioning and gives beer a soft, clean texture, without too much body.

Caramel – darkens colour.

Sugar – some beers receive a small amount in the mash to add sweetness but more often cane sugar is added either to the boil or just after, eventually combining with the ale yeast to produce a higher proportion of fermented beer in the finished article. This darker-coloured invert sugar contributes positively to ales that lean towards bitterness and strong taste, because it can impart attractive flavours of its own. Conversely, the textures of many full-bodied and malty ales benefit from the presence of unfermented sugar.

Priming sugar – as sugar helps fermentation, it is sometimes added to living beer at a late stage, even as casks are being racked, to produce carbon dioxide. In Germany, perhaps to get round the *reinheitsgebot*, some beers are given a small amount of wholly or partially unfermented wort (which, of course, contains sugars) during the conditioning period; this is known as 'krausening' the beer.

Large-scale brewing is today a high-tech industry

27

2. Brewing Processes

The age-old process by which barley produces beer has been subject to much research, from the trial-and-error discoveries of primitive man to the latest advances in engineering and scientific thought. In the modern era of constant technological breakthroughs, almost every aspect of brewing has been revolutionized many times over. Yet the fundamentals never change. Most of the breweries launched during the past decade operate – to a degree that might depend on their equipment or on how big they are – in much the same way as they would have done in the 1890s.

Change is most evident among local giants and multinationals. They have resources to invest in new technology that does more with less and enables them to benefit from the economies of scale. Brewing the same beer in enormous quantities, often in different plants or in several far-flung countries under licence, they require consistency above all. On the other hand, someone brewing a few hundred barrels a week – or even five or ten barrels – values hands-on flexibility, whether or not the technology is state of the art.

A brief description of how beer is brewed can do little more than generalize. Even such differences as exist between the two fundamental process, brewing ale and brewing lager, are not absolute. Some ales are now fermented in lager-type vessels and are then given time to mature, while the commercial pressure to bring lager in line with ale and reduce the time taken to brew and store it – to get it to the pub and shops quicker, so money comes in faster – puts a high premium on corner-cutting ingenuity. What follows, therefore, gives merely the outlines.

Prologue

Liquor (water) to be used in the mash is extracted, from spring or tap, in sufficient volume, chemically treated if necessary, and stored ready for use. Malt is likewise prepared by milling, traditionally into particles rough enough to act as a filter when the mash ends. Some of the smaller brewers operating in restricted space receive their malt ready-crushed by the maltster.

A mash tun

Mashing

The word is sometimes used for brewing tea, a similar if less complex process. Crushed malt (analogous to the tea leaves) is mixed in the mash tun with hot, but not actually boiling, water. Such additives as torrefied wheat may also be introduced. The mix then stews at a temperature of around 65 °C (150 °F) for at least one hour. In that time, the starch converts to sugar and the residual malt expands and collects at the bottom of the mash tun (just as tea leaves do in a pot). When brewers are satisfied conversion has taken place, they drain the wort and then sprinkle (sparge) hot water over the spent grains to extract the last drops of goodness, just as you can re-fill an emptied pot of tea and carry on drinking from it.

That describes the simple infusion system of mashing. The big ale brewers of today may crush their malt into powder and, instead of draining it through the spent grains, transfer it to a wort separator that filters it, rather like a coffee percolator. Because filtering takes half as long as draining, the brewery can mash twice as often.

Brewing lager traditionally involves mashing in more than one vessel and at different temperatures. This so-called 'decoction' system gets the optimum return from malt that may not have been fully modified, while dispersing any elements that might harm the beer. The mash starts at a very much lower temperature of under 40 °C (104 °F). At various times, part is transferred to another vessel that heats it to a higher temperature before returning it, and the entire mash ends up in yet another vessel, known by the German word lauter, in which the wort is separated from the spent grains.

Under German law, only malt may be used in the mash. Other countries may supplement the malt with such cereals as maize, rice and wheat that don't produce enzymes and therefore don't need so much extra care.

Boiling

The malt has now done its job, and the next stage involves what could be described as fine-tuning the flavour. The wort drains from the mash tun/lauter tun to a holding vessel, the underback. From there, it is pumped into a vessel commonly referred to as a 'copper' or 'kettle', wherein it is boiled for around 90 minutes, long enough to allow the flavouring or spicing agents to do their work. The most common of these is the hop, of which different varieties may be inserted into the copper at different times. In general, hops used for bittering are added near the beginning of the boil, while aroma hops are kept back until later.

For whirlpools that remove all traces of the hops by centrifuge before the wort passes on, the more compact pelletised hops are required. In the classic brewhouse, the hop leaves are needed to filter the

The interior of a modern brewhouse

wort as it leaves the copper or hopback. To make the wort as clear as possible at this stage, finings made from dried seaweed are added.

Some brewers add hops at the very end: these are immediately swept to the filter bed and contribute to the flavour of the wort as it passes through them. In the brewing cycle, this is the earliest example of the technique known as 'dry hopping' – adding hops to

Adding hops to the wort

beer after the boil. Hops can also be added in this way at various stages while the beer is conditioning and maturing after fermentation. Many breweries dry-hop at the time draught ale is being racked into the cask from which it will ultimately be served, usually adding pre-measured compressed pellets that will settle at the bottom of the cask, along with the yeast sediment, by the time the beer is drawn off in the pub.

Brewing sugar, used by some brewers to help the beer ferment, contributes most powerfully to the ultimate flavour if added to the boil. Some brewers prefer to wait until the boil is over.

Fermentation and Conditioning

After the boil, the wort collects and is cooled in stages, to just under 20 °C (70 °F) for ale or under 10 °C (50 °F) for lager, before being transferred to the fermenting vessel into which yeast in liquid form is pitched. Times vary, but the very active ale fermentation, during which the conversion of the wort into alcohol leads to much frothing on the surface and an enticing spread of fruity aromas, takes about three days, plus another three days for attenuation, when any remaining fermentable sugars are converted and the beer starts to mature in this less volatile atmosphere. At the end, most of the yeast lies encrusted at the top of the vessel. The beer now requires another few days to condition in a separate tank (perhaps more for stronger or specialist beers) before packaging.

Fermentation

Maturation tanks

Lager takes much longer. Primary fermentation, now increasingly carried out in closed conical vessels, lasts for up to two weeks. Compared with ale, the level of activity at the lower temperature is less pronounced, as the yeast sinks to the bottom. The beer is then transferred to the storage (lagering) tanks where, in temperatures around freezing point, it matures for weeks, even months.

Before they are ready to be packaged, beers may undergo further processing. Filtration removes all or most traces of yeast, while pasteurization sterilizes the beer. In both cases, the removal of yeast means the beer is no longer 'alive', because it has stopped producing carbon dioxide. CO_2 has to be added to preserve the beer until the keg is tapped or the bottle or can opened.

Packaging

In the UK, a substantial amount of bulk beer leaves the brewery in living form, so that the final version of the beer is not determined until the moment of drinking. Barrels carrying it are referred to as casks: hence the term 'cask-conditioned' defines beer that continues to ferment as it leaves the brewery and while it sits in the cellar of the pub, cafe or restaurant. Because the finished article needs to be clear in the glass, finings in liquid form, made traditionally from the swimbladders of sturgeons, are poured in at the racking stage before the cask is sealed. These finings enable all the sediment to sink to the bottom of the cask once it has been made ready for serving. Some brewers also dry-hop the beer in the cask to impart a final touch of flavour.

Casks containing beer that has been filtered and/or pasteurized are known as kegs – the shapes may be identical (in that an increasing number of 'casks' are kept upright in the cellar, as are all kegs), but the essentials differ. Living beer needs containers with an orifice from which excess CO_2 can escape, otherwise the cask would eventually blow up. Beer wholly conditioned in the brewery requires an inlet for the gas cylinder that will help raise it to the bar.

Beer not packaged in bulk goes into bottles or cans. The growing popularity of beer for home consumption has been founded on packs of cans, but

A variety of packaging is available across product ranges

bottled products have retained their position in many countries, and have notably regained some of their former stature in the UK, mainly at the top end of the market. Compared to the time when UK brewers sold considerable amounts of bottled beer in their own pubs, usually to be mixed with draught beer, and expected the empties back, most of the trade today is away from the pub and in non-returnable bottles.

The end result!

BEER ON THE TABLE

The variety of beer available has never been greater. Many pubs now offer a range of both draught and bottled beers whereas once the majority would have been restricted to products from one firm. More and more cafes and restaurants are striving to broaden their portfolios. As for the take-home trade, from major supermarkets to corner off-licences, the big-selling, (usually) canned beers of the larger manufacturers are balanced by bottles from the craft breweries.

Choosing

Beer makes an excellent counterpoint to food, as many now recognize. It rivals wine in both variety and complexity of flavour, and is likewise great for cooking.

Firstly, though, what do you choose when going out just for a drink? A broad rule of thumb in pubs or their equivalents would be stick to local brews. In the UK, Germany, the Czech Republic and the USA that often means beers served on draught (see 'The Tourist Perspective', p.53–67). Not that long ago, these would be divided between a few national brand names and those brewed in or near the region. Today, draught beers from even very small breweries may turn up anywhere in the UK. In general, try those brewed nearby first, as they should be in prime condition – perhaps more so than if you encounter them in some other part of the country (though see the section on keeping and serving beer on p.44).

When buying beer in bottles or cans to drink at home, you may wish to consider how well they might go with food,

Stout and oysters, an age-old combination

whether put in the meal or accompanying it. Stouts, porters and old ales are obvious choices for stews, as are strong ales such as Duvel or Liberty Ale. For game, you could try Belgian reds or browns. Full-bodied pale ales or lagers with touch of hoppy bitterness are ideal for pork, as are wheat beers for sausages, while the more rounded pilseners, suitably chilled, go well with fish. For most puddings, a lambic-based fruit beer should do the trick, followed perhaps by a gueuze or a straight lambic with the cheese.

Similar choices are possible today when eating out. In particular, restaurants specializing in a particular country's cuisine will often carry such beers as Cobra or Kingfisher (Indian) and Tsingtao or Sun Lik (Chinese). As more pubs take pains over the meals they serve, so it makes sense to wash these down with the appropriate beer.

Keeping and serving

When pale ales were shipped from Britain to India during the 19th century, they were brewed to survive a sea voyage of several months without the benefit of temperature control. That meant being very heavily hopped to prevent infection, and brewed to a high gravity. By the time the troops got round to drinking the beer, both the bitterness and the alcoholic strength would have reduced to more normal levels.

Storing beer nowadays may have become much more scientific, but that depends upon everyone involved taking the right kind of care. In the past decade or so, there has been a quiet revolution among brewing companies, perhaps as a result of complaints from the people who drink their beers. Most store their beers at the right temperature, in the brewery and on their delivery drays, and ensure that wholesalers and importers do the same. Bulk beer in casks or kegs as served in on-licensed premises should therefore be drinkable whatever the distance travelled. Brewers are less able to control what happens to bottles and cans once they reach the shops. The dark tint of the bottles offers some protection against bright lights, but shelves in retail outlets are likely to

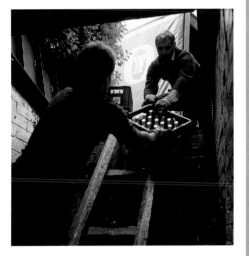

be warm, especially during summer months. If you do not intend to drink beer on the date of purchase, think about where you should store it. A traditional cellar, if you have one, is obviously recommended. Otherwise, find somewhere cool and dark for the beer to stay relatively undisturbed until ready to be chilled and drunk. Most beers have a recommended 'drink by' date of up to a year from bottling or canning, though of course you don't have to wait so

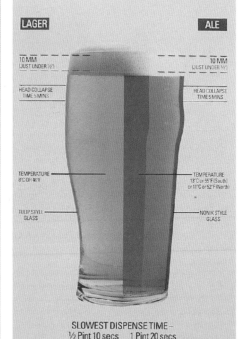

THE PERFECT PINT

LAGER

ALE

10 MM
(JUST UNDER ½")

10 MM
(JUST UNDER ½")

HEAD COLLAPSE
TIME 5 MINS

HEAD COLLAPSE
TIME 5 MINS

TEMPERATURE
8°C or 46°F

TEMPERATURE
13°C or 55°F (South)
or 11°C or 52°F (North)

TULIP STYLE
GLASS

NONIK STYLE
GLASS

SLOWEST DISPENSE TIME –
½ Pint 10 secs   1 Pint 20 secs

long, and the bottle or can may also give advice on storing and serving. Beers that condition in the bottle should stand still and upright for at least 24 hours before being opened to allow the sediment to settle: otherwise, the beer will be cloudy when you pour it and the taste may correspondingly lose a bit of its sparkle – but this does not apply to wheat beers that are intended to remain cloudy.

Lagers are best served at temperatures under 10 °C (50 °F), whereas the temperature recommended for ales is around 12 °C (55 °F). As to how long beer should be chilled before drinking, that obviously depends on the starting temperature. In general, it's better to err on the side of coldness, which probably means allowing ales at least an hour in the refrigerator; when poured, they can be always be left to stand in the glass for a minute or so, or perhaps warmed in the hand, to let the flavour come through. Lagers usually need several hours of chilling.

After removing the top, let the bottle stand for a few seconds for the gas to escape and, especially with bottle-conditioned beers, watch the neck. If the bubbles grow and move upwards, the head as you pour will probably foam right out of the glass and you may prefer to wait, or perhaps even scoop out some of the froth before you continue pouring.

Recently, a trend has caught on for people to be seen drinking straight from the bottle and, we are told, thereby making a 'lifestyle statement'; an alternative interpretation is that they know and care little about beer. Admittedly, with some of the light-weight lagers they are not missing very much. Most bottled beers, though, are crafted to be poured into a glass for the head to form, for excess gas to dissipate at leisure and for flavour to travel smoothly from front to back of the tongue. 'Lifestyle' addicts get the gas and the beer in a series of gulps: on no account should they attempt doing this with beer that conditions in the bottle.

Tasting

The idea of sniffing beer, letting the tongue sample it, spitting it out and then repeating the process would have struck the average miner or foundry worker of former days as a mite eccentric. They took the complexity of flavours beer has always possessed very much for granted although, as brewers and publicans over the years can testify, seasoned drinkers from every background have always been quick to notice and to pass comment whenever the taste of their favourite tipple changes.

We are now familiar with the sight of televised pundits licking their lips and rolling their eyes after trying out a good beer. In print and over the airwaves, a vocabulary of terms has been developed to describe the taste. Both adulatory and unflattering, it expands the vocabulary brewers have long employed to evaluate their own products, and has been popularised in a form that enables technicians and consumers to speak, very broadly, the same language.

Beer can aspire to a complexity that deserves a considered approach, even if you avoid the full-blown antics of professional tasters, which if nothing else waste valuable drinking time. Several years ago, the brewing industry proposed for its own use a flavour terminology made up of 44 generic terms, plus a further 78 to identify individual flavours. The generic terms ranged from technical ('acetaldehyde') to demotic ('catty') and were grouped together into 14 primary classes, each with subsidiaries, in the form of a mnemonic chart, called the Flavour Wheel.

Quality Assurance managers conduct taste panels to ensure the perfect pint

Such terms as fruity, nutty, and burnt – the first two in general being complimentary, the last less so – imply further subdivisions tasters can use as they gain experience. The tasting process itself divides roughly into four stages: smell, taste, texture (mouthfeel) and aftertaste. Before drinking, sniff the beer then check out the colour (if it comes from a bottle, try to sniff before and after you pour). Apart from anything else, this helps prepare the tastebuds for what follows and, in unfortunate cases, can warn you against beer in poor condition.

When you first sip the beer, roll it around your tongue and allow the texture and taste to register before swallowing. Sometimes, flavours change or grow more pronounced as the beer goes down, not least because your 'bitterness' tastebuds are found towards the back of the tongue. The heavy 'vinous' taste (the comparison is more with port or sherry than wines) of strong dark beers and barley wines heralds a pleasingly warm sensation after imbibing.

How many glasses?

The medical aspect of this question lies outside the scope of this book, whose readers are referred to whatever the experts currently recommend. To make sense of any advice on safety levels regarding alcohol consumption, it does help to know the alcoholic strength of what you propose to drink. In the UK, at any rate, all bottles and cans should display this, as do

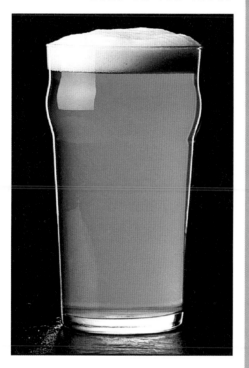

many pump-clips in the pub (though lager and processed-beer dispense fonts are less helpful).

Strength in the UK is usually expressed in terms of alcohol by volume (ABV). A beer of 3.5% ABV contains 3.5 parts alcohol to every 100 parts of water in the finished product. Obviously, the higher the figure, the more alcohol is in the beer and, on a strict measure-for-measure comparison, the quicker it takes effect. As with safe drinking levels, so are the descriptive terms commonly employed in the trade hard to define precisely. As a rough guide, the strength of standard beers rises to about 4.0% ABV, while Premium beers range between 4.0% and 5.0% ABV. Beyond that, there are strong beers and barley wines, the latter usually between 7.0% and 10.0% ABV.

THE TOURIST PERSPECTIVE

First, a definition: for the purposes of this book, any beer stored in bulk – cask, keg or tank – to be consumed in a pub, or similar licensed premises, will be described as draught beer. This includes beers that undergo secondary fermentation in the cellar and beers that the brewery has conditioned before despatch.

In 1995, 65% of the beer consumed in the UK was on draught, compared to 35% in cans or bottles (the ratio has not changed since then). Of the other major beer-producing nations, the Czech Republic ranked next in terms of draught beer consumption with 44%, followed by Belgium and Luxembourg with 39%, Spain with 35% and Austria with 33%. No other country which brewed more than 10 million hectolitres (1760 million pints) of beer per year exceeded 30%. In the three biggest beer producers, the proportions of draught beer consumption were 11% for the USA, 2% for China, and 22% for Germany. Significantly, draught beer drinkers did not necessarily look for strong beers: the average strength in the UK was 4.0% ABV, compared to the Czechs with 4.3%, although Belgium, Spain and Austria were above average with beers of 5.0% ABV.

Draught beer in most of these countries is highly recommended. There are many small breweries and brewpubs, and some of their products are only available locally. Tourists who rate the sampling of local food dishes as a high priority should adopt the same inquisitive approach to beer. The different styles, including examples of each, are examined more closely in The Beer Directory, even where the majority of the beer available, as with mild ale in the UK, is produced in bulk.

United Kingdom

The UK tradition of top-fermenting ales, dispensed in a natural state without being filtered or pasteurized, has survived. Although not widely adopted elsewhere, brewers in other countries have emulated British real ale, just as some of the newer breed of UK breweries

have tried their hand at lagers, wheat beers and other foreign styles. Whatever their size, all UK breweries produce beers of standard strengths – described loosely as 'bitters', though the degree of bitterness varies enormously, with a few acknowledged as 'milds' - that are considered weak enough for the equivalent of several pints to be consumed in a session.

Regional variations today are not clear-cut. Many breweries closed between 1950 and 1970, while beers developed by recent arrivals have rarely been based on local recipes. An exception can be found in Scotland, where the tradition of full-bodied, slightly sweet ales was kept alive by Belhaven in Dunbar and the Scottish-Courage brewery in Edinburgh and revived by Caledonian when it took over the Lorimer & Clark brewery, also in Edinburgh.

In Southern England, breweries near the hop fields of Kent and Sussex go for strongly aromatic flavours, as found in many

A traditional sign-writer

beers by Shepherd Neame, Harvey and King & Barnes. In the Midlands, the Black Country to the west of Birmingham remains a bastion of mild and of draught bitters which are sweeter than average. Two of the

smallest breweries surviving from the Victorian era, Holden and Batham, own a clutch of pubs, and their excellent beers, almost all on draught, rarely travel far.

The same applies to those breweries in and around Manchester. Flavours tend to be dry and sharp, as found in the intensely bitter beers of Holt's, which are generally confined to the locality. As a centre of brewing famous for water, high in sulphates, that set the standard for IPA, Burton upon Trent is noted for draught Bass and, especially, for Marston's Pedigree, a beer that still ferments in casks designed to release the surplus yeast. Marston's is a large regional brewer with a national presence, as are Wadworth with 6X (malty, sweetish) and Morland with Old Speckled Hen (bitingly hoppy), both of which enjoy widespread distribution.

All the breweries mentioned so far run tied houses, as do most of their older-established colleagues. Some of those formed in the last twenty years are brewpubs, with at least one guaranteed outlet, or own a handful of pubs. For the bulk of their sales, though, most rely on the free trade, generally a mix between selling a beer locally on a regular basis and joining the guest-beer market, where a beer is on sale in a particular pub for a very limited period before it is replaced by another. In such cases, the beer may be a one-off creation, unlikely to be repeated in the same form unless the initial brew creates a demand. Some pubs feature a regular series of individually-brewed guest beers. Beers are often produced for a specific event, which can range in size from the national festival organised by the Campaign for Real Ale to beer festivals run by a single pub. Seasonal beers have also become increasingly common

These are all beers that undergo a secondary fermentation in the cask. However, most of the draught sold in UK pubs is conditioned at the brewery. Such major lager brands as Heineken, Carlsberg, Castlemaine and Fosters are brewed under licence with the strength kept low to encourage mass consumption. Lager has recently been joined by the current sensation: fairly strong brewery-conditioned ales kept cool, dispensed by a mixed-gas (mainly nitroogen) pressure system and known colloquially as 'nitrokegs' or 'smooths'. They are reliable but hard to enthuse over compared to the traditional product when served at its best.

Germany

Germany comes third behind the USA and China as a beer producer and is second only to the Czech Republic in per capita consumption. Yet by world standards it doesn't have many enormous brewing combines, and it exports only a modest proportion of its total production, though still more than other nations can manage. Germany's strength lies in its home market and in its number of breweries which, at over 1000, is matched only by the USA.

Traditional German beer tankards

Although only a quarter of the beer sold in Germany is on draught, from a yearly total of nearly 120,000 million hectolitres (21,216,760 million pints) that leaves plenty of foaming mugs sold across the counter. Two styles of beer in particular – both top-fermenting in a land noted for its pilseners and dark lagers – are not widely available outside Germany and are best sampled at a bar in the city where they are brewed, sometimes even on the premises. Brewers in Cologne have exclusive rights to produce the pale refreshing Kolschbier - just as with certain French wines, beers of that name must come from Cologne and nowhere else. The Düsseldorf equivalents of the British brewpubs all brew the famous *altbier*, a darkish ale, malty but with bitterness, and dispensed straight from the cask.

Many cities have at least one brewpub but most of these are located in Bavaria, which is not surprising as Bavaria contains more than half of Germany's breweries. Two of the region's specialities are wheat beers (also a speciality of Berlin) and the smoked beers associated with the town of Bamberg, but all kinds and colours of mainly bottom-fermented beer are available, often intended for drinking on the premises and not exported much further than the next village, if that far.

United States

Easily the biggest beer revolution of recent years has occurred in the USA. Having spent several decades contracting the industry into a few large firms, of which Anheuser-Busch is by far the biggest in the world, it now rivals Germany in the number of breweries. There are few identifiable regional trends, but every beer style in the world is brewed somewhere in the USA. Often, these are given a distinctive twist through the inspired use of local ingredients, notably the highly aromatic American-grown hops.

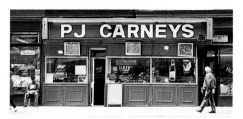

A typical New York bar

Already brewing more beer than any other country, the USA increased production by more than 50% between 1970 and 1990. Because it is so vast, even the heavily advertised brands do not seem as all-pervasive as in the UK, and brewpubs or restaurants can survive by stocking just their own products. Conversely, few of the new breweries, some of them quite substantial operations, have developed a truly national – let alone an international – presence.

Most parts of the USA are now well supplied with breweries. The German brewing tradition, strong in a country once very open to German immigrants, perhaps influenced both the widespread use of high-grade equipment and the unwillingness to cut corners. Whereas most microbreweries in the UK produce beer that conditions in the cask, American draught beer is often filtered and dispensed under pressure. Average strength is higher than in the UK; the concept of 'session beers' of under 4.0% ABV that are intended to be consumed in vast amounts seems foreign to American practice.

Czech Republic

Apart from the UK, no country consumes a higher proportion of its beer on draught than the Czech Republic. Czechs also drink more beer per head than anyone else and, as the world's first gold-coloured lager came from Pilsen, the town that gave its name to the brand, the republic's eminence can hardly be overestimated. Other styles are brewed, but pilseners still dominate.

Pilsner Urquell and Budweiser Budvar, the two most famous brands, are among those widely available on draught. The departed Communist governments of Eastern Europe have little to boast about but, partly through inertia, the former Czech regime protected the age-old traditions, in that beer continued to ferment for long periods in traditional

vessels and was generally cared for in ways that accountants, of the kind increasingly influential in large Western breweries, would certainly have changed. Since then, Pilsner Urquell has switched to steel conical fermenters and we await the future of the Budvar brewery, complicated by its battles with Anheuser-Busch over the Budweiser name, with fingers tightly crossed.

Belgium

Of the great brewing nations, Belgium more than the others tends to offer its finest products in packaged form. Draught beer may account for 40% of sales in Belgium but much of this consists of pils-style lagers, some excellent but hardly what Belgium is most famous for.

Huisbroouwerij Straffe Hendrik, a restored 16th-century brewery in Bruges run by the Henri Maes Company (above and opposite)

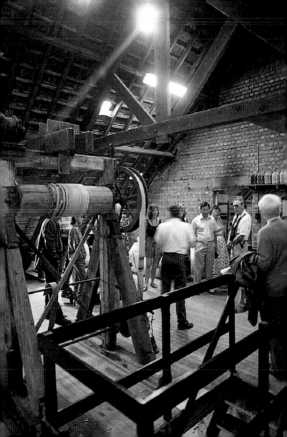

In Brussels, there are bars serving draught beers of lambic derivation, including krieks and other fruit-flavoured beers. Hoegaarden is widely available and around Antwerp, which is full of outstanding drinking haunts, the local De Koninck is served on tap (in the famous *bolleke* glass). There are a few brewpubs. However, whereas visitors to the countries mentioned earlier should 'think draught', in Belgium check first what is on offer. Most bars carry a good selection of indigenous bottled beers, some of which may be hard to find abroad.

The Rest

Canada, Japan, Finland, Northern France (near the Belgian border) and Australasia form a disparate collection of countries in which there is a fair chance of finding a brewpub. China obviously has great potential, though its consumption per head is low and most beer is packaged. For general beer tourism, the Netherlands has the most prestigious selection of bars that stock quality products from around the world.

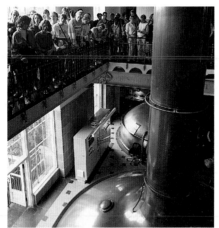

Visitors at the world-famous Carlsberg brewery in Copenhagen (above and opposite)

BEER TODAY

INTRODUCTION

Which is the sexiest alcoholic beverage in the world? The one you most enjoy watching your favourite television personality or film star posing with? That beer can even be thought of as a candidate nowadays proves how much it's image has become more upmarket. A one-time drink of the toiling masses, consumed most often in dives or on the factory floor, now stands on the shelves of all the smartest shops and supermarkets in designer bottles, and sometimes to designer recipes.

Of course, beer has had to change. The size of the working classes in Western countries has shrunk, not least because manual jobs have either disappeared or been transformed beyond recognition. The industrial tradition of working up a thirst down the mines or in some oven-like foundry, after which huge quantities of beer could be consumed without effort (or commensurate ill effects), has disappeared from many countries. At the same time, modern lifestyles revolve increasingly around dietary and health

68

Designer ads for designer beers: John Smith Bitter
(opposite), Newcastle Brown Ale and McEwan's Export

concerns, in which a knowledge of alcoholic strength and safe levels of consumption is important. Laws discouraging drink-driving have also grown more stringent.

While beer lost a significant part of its traditional captive audience, wine became heavily marketed as a universal drink, rather than the preserve of wine-growing countries or the more affluent diners, and appealed to the emergent middle classes. An example of how beer is fighting back can be seen in the number of speciality bottled beers sold in the UK, for which the figures suggest a threefold increase between 1985 and 1995, much of the growth coming in the last two years. Ten years ago, even medium-sized UK brewers were closing their bottling lines, in some cases not even bothering to have the beers bottled by someone else. Many have rejoined the bottle market, along with several of the new small breweries.

The global scenario has been transformed. Apart from a handful of lagers that were mass-produced on an international scale, each of the major brewing countries kept its beers to itself. Today, drinkers every-where are exposed increasingly to the best on offer, whatever its origins. In particular, some of the great idiosyncratic beers of Belgium, including the sour fruit beers, now sell worldwide – indeed, over a quarter of Belgium's beer production is exported, a ratio exceeded only by Ireland and the Netherlands with their international stout and lager brands.

Based on the number of breweries and beers of the major brewing nations, Germany and Belgium have changed the least, with greater concentration of ownership offset by a revival of traditional products, notably wheat beers. The political turnaround in the Czech Republic has led to famous breweries appointing new managers and being run in different ways.

The biggest upheavals by far have taken place in the United Kingdom and the United States, where there had been a serious danger of a monopolized industry developing, aiming bland beers at the mass market. In 1950, there were about 360 separate brewing companies in the UK, accounting for nearly 570 breweries.

Traquair House in the Scottish Borders, home to a restored 18th-century brewhouse now producing highly distinctive ales

By 1970, the number of companies had shrunk to under 100. Matters improved, and by 1990 the number had increased to nearly 250, rising to 450 in 1995, with around 480 breweries. Most of the beer consumed still comes from a clutch of giant firms. But on the plus side, never before has the public been able to choose between so many different styles of beers from so many brewers so readily - from a shop, or in the bar, cafe or pub. What has happened in these countries has been reflected on a more modest scale elsewhere, notably in Scandinavia and Japan.

The Great British Beer Festival (above and opposite)

The future? While beer consumption is static in much of the Western world, it is expected to grow worldwide by almost 25%, between 1993 and 1998. In the Far East, the figure projected is closer to 70%. Production in China alone rose by nearly 90% in five years, and the Chinese now account for 12% of the world's consumption, second only to the USA – though in both countries consumption per head is below average. Central and South America have seen production more than double in many countries, from Mexico to Argentina.

Both the mass and the specialist markets will continue to thrive on change - this will involve on the one hand successors to such trends as Mexican lagers or fruit beers and a further range of higher-quality products, and on the other, an ever-changing selection of beers, especially on draught, will be targeted at the connoisseurs as a means of keeping them interested in beer and tempting them out of doors and into the pubs, themselves being transformed from the low-life, male-dominated drinking dens of the past. In recent years, the number of individual draught beers newly introduced by UK brewers has been averaging about 1000 each year. Bars, pubs and restaurants that brew their own beer are proliferating in the USA and the UK and are spreading throughout Japan.

Change is not always for the better, however. Two classic beers highlighted in this book, Samiclaus and Imperial Russian Stout, are not currently being brewed. Those responsible may be persuaded to reverse their decision, or perhaps give other companies the rights to brew, not least because the best of the established beers and those brewers that have battled through to continue to produce them are now regarded as prime national assets, supported by organisations within the industries and by consumer movements, of which the British Campaign for Real Ale has had the most spectacular success. Wherever, you are, these are interesting times for beer lovers.

Cheers!

THE BEER DIRECTORY

The Beer Directory seeks to classify the main styles of beer and give detailed examples, including the name of the beer, the country of origin, its brewery, alcoholic strength of beer (expressed by Alcohol By Volume – ABV), and a brief description. Questions of flavour, appearance and quality are all, to some extent, subjective and, especially in cases where the beer re-ferments in the bottle, the taste itself may undergo changes while the bottle is on the shelf.

While the strength indicated should give a true guide as to the nature of the beer and be reasonably accurate, brewers sometimes adjust this, perhaps when redesigning the label or finding other ways to relaunch the beer. Some beers, Orval being an example, grow stronger by the years as the yeast in the bottle does its work.

Many of the beers featured are available as both draught (especially in their home countries) and bottled beers. Sometimes, there may be differences between draught and bottled versions. The text does not make always make these distinctions but, with the exception of some British ales, all beers can be assumed to exist in bottled form.

If a beer is bottle-conditioned, this is clearly spelled out in some cases, but bottled beers may, now or in the future, exist in both forms (i.e. some versions may be brewery-conditioned). In most cases, where the bottle contains live yeast, the label should indicate this; however, there will be exceptions, just as not all labels in all countries include the strength of beer.

LAGERS

American Lager

The most widely available beers in the USA, as produced by its biggest brewers, are of the kind described in the section on pale lagers (see p.98). One result of the US microbrewery revolution that

has adopted all beer styles, often adding new characteristics, has been the revival of what are sometimes referred to as 'red' or 'amber' lagers. Almost certainly inspired by the Vienna style, these were drunk enthusiastically in the big cities before Prohibition.

Today, an increasing number of lagers from companies of all sizes have a deep amber or light

Brooklyn Lager
(USA) • 5.1% ABV

red colour and, sometimes, a soft texture, though the brewers are less likely to aim for Vienna's smooth, malty flavour. In the case of Brooklyn Lager (ABV 5.1%), for instance, the powerful tang of hops and the bitter-sweet aftertaste are clearly intentional.

'Malt liquor' is an American description, one of those odd terms (rather like the British adoption of barley wine) for a lager that is stronger than the norm

77

but otherwise has few identifiable characteristics. Despite the name, malt does not figure as the key component of the wort, nor does it register strongly in the final taste. The aim is to produce a strong lager as seamlessly as possible, which usually involves adding plenty of brewing sugar to bump up fermentation. At around 6.0% ABV or more, there is enough strength to

give the finished article some body. Most of the big breweries offer examples, such as King Cobra, Colt 45 and Red Bull. In addition, all beers over a certain strength are referred to as 'malt liquors' in some states.

Roscoe's Red

Brewery	Anheuser-Busch
Strength (ABV)	5.0%
Description	Amber-red colour. Fruity aroma, with hint of perfume. Quite smooth, with a sweetish malty flavour and nutty aftertaste.

Red Bull

Brewer	Stroh
Strength (ABV)	7%
Description	Pale-golden colour. Quite full, oily texture with a nutty flavour that stays to the end.

Black beer

A German speciality, this can be regarded as the lager equivalent of stout or porter. In colour, black lagers are at least as dark as the Bavarian dunkels; in taste, they have the chocolate-flavoured bitterness of stout, though in a smoother, more rounded form.

Within the former East Germany, the style has been kept going by a brewery in the spa town of Köstritz, Thüringen. Since re-unification, Köstritzer Schwarzbier, with a strength of 4.6% ABV, has not only become more widespread but has inspired something of a fad for *schwarzbiers* within Germany, even if of the more usual dark-lager type.

A long way from Thüringen, black beers in a similar tradition are produced by the major brewers of Japan – Asahi, Kirin, Sapporo and Suntory – though all put more commercial effort into their lighter-coloured lagers. The existence of these beers can be traced to the German impact on Asian brewing techniques. In another part of the world, the same probably applies to Xingu, a very dark lager from Brazil.

Köstritzer Schwarzbier	
Brewery	Köstritzer
Strength (ABV)	4.6%
Description	Dark brown colour. Chewy texture, with malty, roasted chocolate flavour leading to a bitter-coffee finish.

Bock

The German tradition of brewing beers to last long journeys – similar to the British IPAs of Burton upon Trent – survives in the town of Einbeck, to the west of Berlin and just south of Braunschweig (Brunswick). Once more important than its present modest state would suggest, Einbeck made beers deliberately strong to survive travel, or to be stored for several months. These would have been top-fermenting, but today the term 'bock' (a contraction of 'Einbock', as the name is pronounced locally) is

Superbock (Portugal)
• 5.8% ABV

commonly used to indicate a malt-tasting, bottom-fermenting beer of at least 6.0% ABV.

For a couple of centuries, these have been mostly associated with Munich and the surrounding area. Bocks may be light or dark in colour. They were often conceived as seasonal beers,

Gulpener Bock

Brewery	Gulpener
Strength (ABV)	6.5%
Description	Citric-pear aroma. Sweet, full, malty flavour. Slight molasses-bitter aftertaste.

either to be drunk at springtime or to be sampled during the non-brewing summer months. Several continue to use the term 'Maibock' in the title, signifying a spring or May beer.

Bock means 'goat' in German. The Dutch equivalent is often spelt 'bok', a term (and a beer) that once nearly died out but has revived in the last decade or so – to the extent that Netherland boks are probably more widely available than the German beers they (somewhat) resemble in name and character. The seasonal element comes through in the spring *meibok*, Grolsch Meibok being an example. However, the more common Dutch *bokbier* tends to be dark and is intended to be drunk later in the year, when summer is over. To complicate matters, some boks are top-fermenting ales, including a strong (7.0% ABV) Meibok by Brand.

Hubertusbock

Brewery	Hacker-Pschorr
Strength (ABV)	6.5%
Description	Copper colour. Rich fruity aroma, full texture, well-balanced mix of malt with a citric hoppiness that lasts to the end.

Dark Lagers

Before the technical innovations that led, eventually, to bottom-fermented (i.e. lager-type) beers becoming the world's most popular style and renowned for their pale colour, most beers were dark. This would have been true of lagers then brewed in Bavaria, which today – especially Munich and the northern area around Bamberg and Bayreuth – remains a centre of their production.

Most of the bigger brewers include a so-called *Dunkel* (German for 'dark') in their product range, though the growth in demand for the paler lagers, more heavily promoted and exported far more widely, tended to overshadow them until recently. In general, they aim for a malty, sweetish base, balanced by a slight edge to the aftertaste thanks to a generous dose of hops. Strength averages 5.5% ABV.

Credited with inventing, or at least perfecting the style, Munich's Spaten brewery still produces a dunkel, as do Paulaner (probably the darkest in

Ayinger Dunkel	
Brew	Ayinger
Strength (ABV)	5.2%
Description	Red-brown colour. Quite sharp, malty taste with hint of chocolate.

colour), Hacker-Pschorr, Augustiner and Ayinger. To the north, one of the area's most charismatic brewers, Prince Luitpold of Bavaria, whose castle houses the Kaltenberg brewery, is proud of his König Ludwig Dunkel, named after his great-grandfather, who happened to be king of Bavaria.

Among leading Franconian brewers, Maisel from Bayreuth brew a Dunkel, as do EKU from Bamberg. The classic comes from the Kulmbach, where Kulmbacher Mönchshof's (so named because the brewery occupies a former monastery) Kloster Schwarz Bier is both weaker, at 4.7% ABV, and hoppier than the norm. Over the border in the Czech Republic, there is a similar tradition of dark lagers, including those from Regent and Staropramen. As in Germany, some notable examples come from local breweries and brewpubs whose beers can only be sampled close to home. The style is international: American brewers, including the giant Anheuser-Busch, brew tasty examples, although these are less commercially successful than the paler products.

Staropramen Dark

Brewer	Staropramen
Strength (ABV)	4.6%
Description	Brown-red colour. Nutty aroma. Smooth texture, roasted malt flavour with chocolate overtones, persisting to the finish.

Doppelbock

Not to be taken literally, the term *Doppelbok* ('double-bock') describes a bock that is stronger than the norm of around 6.0% ABV. The most famous brand has a monastery past, and it seems the practice of brewing strong beers for drinking during Lent as a food substitute may have be the inspiration of this style.

Munich's Paulaner brewery, started as a monastery dedicated to St Francis of Paula. In the 17th century,

the locals were able to buy their powerful Salvator ('saviour'), which is still brewed there at a strength of 7.5% ABV and timed to hit the streets in the period before Easter.

Paulaner Salvator (Germany)
• 7.5% ABV

Paulaner lost its monastic status a

Andechs Doppelbock Dunkel

Brewery	Kloster Andechs
Strength (ABV)	7.0%
Description	Brown-red colour. Sharp, fruity aroma. Full, sweetish taste, slightly caramelly, but also with roastiness. Sweet aftertaste.

couple of centuries ago, but the trend set by this full-bodied and nicely balanced beer continues, with most of Salvator's competitors coming up with similar names. Hacker-Pschorr's Animator, Ayinger's Fortunator and Löwenbräu's Triumphator are among the rivals. North of Munich, the EKU brewery in Kulmbach brews a Kulminator and tops that with its Kulminator 28. Of those beers produced regularly, this is one of the world's strongest, at 12.0% ABV.

Doppelbocks tend to be on the dark side of pale: an example marketed as Doppelbock Dunkel is brewed by Kloster ('cloister') Andechs, south of Munich, the

name serving as a reminder of the beer's monastic heritage. In the Netherlands, home of the autumnal boks, Brand brew a Dubbelbok.

Kulminator 28

Brewer	EKU
Strength (ABV)	12.0%
Description	Amber-gold colour. Heavy fruit aroma. Very warming, malt-dominated flavour with a powerful fruity finish.

Dry and Lite Beers

In North America and Japan, the producers of mass-marketed pale lagers have often concentrated on beers intended to make a cool, crisp and clean impact. Strong flavours rank lower in importance. Ice beers provide one example: another arose from the development of so-called 'dry beers' by Asahi in Japan. A special yeast is used and, after a thorough fermentation, the beer is cold-filtered to remove most of the unwanted flavours (notably any hoppiness) that might linger on the palate. The dry, clean aftertaste is a notable feature.

Cold filtration also originated in Japan. Although the alcoholic content is unchanged by this process, it has some similarities with ice beer (see p.86) insofar as cold temperatures help to filter out the yeast and

Miller Genuine Draft (USA) • 4.7% ABV

other matter left over from fermentation. As a result, there is no need to pasteurize. Another example widely available is Miller's Genuine Draft.

'Lite' or 'light' in the USA indicates that a beer is low in calories and specifies its calorie content on the bottle. They are usually little above 4.0% ABV or well below it, and they are part of most of the major brewers' portfolios; examples include Miller Lite, Coors Light. Removing some of the more robust ingredients of beer in the interest of weight-watching does, of course, take something from the taste, but they do go down easily enough.

Asahi Super Dry	
Brewer	Asahi
Strength (ABV)	5.0%
Description	Very pale. Faint pear aroma. Light, fruity taste, smooth, slightly oily, very dry finish with a hint of almonds.

Eisbock/Ice beers

The German term *Eisbock* ('ice-bock') is the trademark of a beer from the Reichelbräu brewery of Kulmbach, in northern Bavaria. It describes the technique of freezing the beer while it ferments. Because water has a higher freezing point than alcohol, the removal of ice from the fermenting vessel will increase the proportion of alcohol, thereby producing a stronger beer without the problems inherent in fermenting beers of a high gravity.

The malt grist for Reichelbräu's Eisbock includes one variety that has the deliberate function of preventing excessive sweetness in the final product. This emerges with 10.0% ABV, a darkish red colour and a well-balanced, cafe-creme flavour.

More commonly available in the world's markets are the various ice beers originating from Canada, a country familiar with icy conditions but perhaps inspired by the German example. In fact, all the major US brewers produce their own versions. In general, they are strongish (between 5% and 6% ABV), smooth and clean-tasting, though without much character.

Carlsberg Ice Beer
(Denmark)
• 5.6% ABV

Labatts Ice Beer (Canada)
• 5.6% ABV

Kulmbacher Eisbock

Brewery	Reichelbräu
Strength (ABV)	10.0%
Description	Brown-red colour. Full texture, strong malty flavour with a slightly bitter, roasted aftertaste.

Canadian Ice

Brewery	Molson
Strength (ABV)	5.5%
Description	Yellow colour. Light pear aroma. Full, slightly oily texture, citric tang that carries on to the sweetish aftertaste.

Export

Another local style of restricted availability elsewhere – which is ironic, given the name – Export comes from Dortmund. In appearance, it resembles a pilsener but is smoother and less bitter. Not especially malty, it has the full body associated with beers that deliberately contain non-fermentable sugars. Average strength is around 5.5% ABV.

DAB Export

Brewer	DAB
Strength (ABV)	5.0%
Description	Light colour. Malty flavour, slightly sweet, with hops coming through in the aftertaste

These Exports were obviously made to travel. Still one of Germany's major brewing cities, such major firms as DAB and DUB produce lagers galore but tend to confine the beer for which Dortmund is internationally famous among connoisseurs to home territory. There, it is widespread, the element of local pride underlined by the fact that all brewers include the Dortmunder name as part of their corporate identity.

Whereas the conjunction of 'Dortmunder' and 'Export' on a label proves authenticity, some brewers appropriate the Export title for lagers sent abroad, one of the most common being Binding's Export Privat (5.3% ABV). These on the whole follow the spirit of the originals (only Exports from Dortmund are entitled to incorporate the city's name), as do some recent examples from the USA. However, ales and wheat beers may also be called Export. Outside Germany, the description 'Dort' indicates a close relation, Gulpener's Dort from the Netherlands being an example.

Light/Low

The North American term 'lite' or 'light' refers to beers that are low in calories and specify their calorie content on the bottle. These are covered under the section on dry and lite beers (see p.86). Confusingly, in other countries the term usually refers to the alcohol content: the Australian Swan Light (1.0% ABV), for example . In Sweden and other Scandinavian countries, light beers tend to be under 3.0% ABV, often higher than those so classified in other countries, where anything much over 1.0% ABV would not qualify them for this category.

Swan Light (Australia)
• 1.0% ABV

Beers that do qualify are described as low-alcohol or non-alcoholic /alcohol-free. Sometimes, the brewing technique is conventional, then alco-

Kaliber (Ireland)
• 0.05% ABV

hol is removed; at other times, there is very little alcohol to begin with. One alcohol-free beer that is brewed normally is Kaliber, from Guinness.

St Christopher (UK) • 0.05% ABV

Both kinds enjoyed a boom a few years ago and are still around in some quantities. Their original purpose may have been to cash in on the increasingly stringent drink-driving regulations by enabling beer-drinkers to consume several glasses and still be able to drive without breaking the law. If the rounded flavours imparted by alcohol tend to be absent, there are some compensations, especially for those who enjoy beer but have to restrict their alcoholic intake.

Clausthaler

Brewery	Binding
Strength (ABV)	0.5%
Description	Low-alcohol beer. Pale colour. Soft, smooth and dry, with a light balance of hops and sweetness.

Märzen

Because of the heat, summer in Europe was traditionally a bad time for brewing. As a result, the practice developed of producing sufficient beer while the climate was cool, storing it and subsequently drawing it from the storage tanks as required. March would have been an obvious month for this intensive brewing activity. The term *Märzen* originated in Munich and was often applied to beers brewed to be drunk during the city's festival in October (the famous *Oktoberfest*). The style of such beer traditionally resembled the malty, reddish lagers first created in Vienna. Beer of this kind which was conditioned for six months at the right temperature would end up with such desirable features as a crisp palate and a full but refreshing taste.

Oktoberfest beers

Oktoberfest beers today are often pale lagers of the kind tourists are expected to lap up, but the darker style lives on, both in Munich and seasonal specialities from elsewhere. Among the more widely available Munich examples are those from Hofbräu and Spaten, whose Ur-Märzen is probably the surviving classic, but smaller breweries dotted around Bavaria still produce amber-red lagers of this kind for local consumption.

Spaten Ur-Märzen

Brewery	Spaten
Strength (ABV)	5.6%
Description	Amber colour. Smooth, malty flavour with just a hint of bitterness that makes all the difference.

THE BEER DIRECTORY

Munich Pale

There is a tradition of pale lagers from Bavaria, where they are often marketed as *Hell*, the German for 'pale'. These may have the smoothness and fullness of texture of a pilsener, but are less bitter, lighter in colour and, on average, slightly weaker. First developed at the end of the nineteenth century, they were overshadowed for several decades by the darker lagers until Munich followed the world and swung more towards light-coloured beers.

By UK standards, the ABV of what are essentially the standard beers of the region remains high, at around 5.0%. Whereas a lower-gravity draught bitter in the UK, aimed at a local market, was sometimes referred to colloquially as 'cooking bitter' or 'boys' bitter', bottles of Bavarian-brewed lager may include the description *vollbier*; this means literally 'full beer', and is a guarantee of strength.

The more substantial firms based in Munich itself – Augustiner, Ayinger, Hacker-Pschorr, Löwenbräu and

---

Löwenbräu Helles

Brewery	Löwenbräu
Strength (ABV)	5.3%
Description	Pale. Smooth and malty, with slightly sweet aftertaste.

Spaten (where the style originated) among them – all produce helles of this kind, as do breweries, large and small, throughout Bavaria. Given the proximity of the Czech Republic, it is hardly surprising that the region brews plenty of pilseners. A growing tendency of consumers to ask for the sharper, usually slightly stronger pils is reflected noticeably in markets overseas, so that major breweries also producing pilseners are likely to put more effort into exporting these.

Augustiner Hell

Brewery	Augustiner
Strength (ABV)	5.2%
Description	Pale. Light fruity aroma. Soft texture, leading to clean malty taste.

Pale Lagers

International brewing combines have relied on pale lagers to attack the world's market. Two of the more ubiquitous are Carlsberg from Denmark and Heineken from the Netherlands. Their beers are often brewed under licence in the country of sale, where the recipes may be adapted to local custom. In the UK, for instance, the extraordinary rise in draught lager consumption was built originally around a product low in alcoholic strength and therefore suitable for drinking in considerable amounts during a single session: the basic lager sold in cans or, especially, on draught was far below the 5.0% ABV of the Dutch Heineken brew or the 4.8% ABV of Carlsberg's leading Danish product.

Carlsberg (Denmark) • 4.8% ABV

Castlemaine XXXX (Australia)
• 4.0% ABV

The more widely dispersed pale lagers – a variegated list that could include Fosters and Castlemaine from Australia, Becks and Holsten from Germany and, increasingly, the biggest Japanese and New Zealand brewers – do not really fall into such categories as pilsener. They may be tailored for export and, in the majority of cases, do not represent

Budweiser

Brewery	Anheuser-Busch
Strength (ABV)	5.0%
Description	Pale, light colour. Smooth texture, clean-tasting with slight fruit undertones.

Tsingtao Beer

Brewery`	Tsingtao
Strength (ABV)	5.0%
Description	Pale, light aroma and texture, light-fruity hoppiness, strong enough to linger in the aftertaste.

Cobra (India) • 5.0% ABV

the most distinctive brand of lager from a particular brewery. In their packaged forms, at least, they usually offer a beer above average in strength and quality.

Mainstream lagers from North America are increasingly being exported and/or brewed overseas under licence. These are almost always pale, clean-tasting and very drinkable without possessing much character. To capitalize on the popularity in the West of such cuisines as Indian and Chinese, certain lagers that originate from these countries are becoming more widespread.

Pilsener

King Wenceslas, celebrated throughout the Western world in the famous Christmas carol, ruled over Bohemia, now part of the Czech Republic. A couple of his heirs have played a role in the development of beer, notably the King Wenceslas who conferred brewing rights upon the town of Pilsen 700 years ago.

The original beer, being dark and opaque, would have borne little relation to a modern pilsener. By 1842, they would have been brewing bottom-fermented lagers in Pilsen when the first golden, see-through, lager-type beer was created. Whether or not this happened by accident, as has been claimed, there is no doubting its impact. Since then, Pilsen has been renowned for the style, and pilseners (often spelled as 'pilsner' or shortened to 'pils') have been produced worldwide.

Bitburger Pils (Germany)
• 4.6% ABV

In the process, the term has been more than somewhat abused by being applied to almost any pale lager. To justify the name, the beer should combine a golden colour (not too pale) with a fairly full body and a soft texture, and be sufficiently well hopped to impart a dry, bitter tang. The classic from Pilsen's own brewery, marketed as Pilsner Urquell ('the original pilsner') remains supreme, even though the large wooden tuns in which the beer used to ferment and then condition at leisure have now been replaced by steel, making the finished product slightly less distinctive.

Pilsner Urquell

Brewer	Pilsner Urquell
Strength (ABV)	4.4%
Description	Golden colour. Enticing citric aroma from the local Saaz hops. Soft texture, bitter background, dominated bY complex fruit flavours.

Outside the Czech Republic, the pale lagers most deserving the name of pilsener come from Bavaria, the former East Germany, and further west in Rhineland, where the best examples have a touch of hop bitterness allied to an appropriately smooth texture. Many pale lagers, whatever merits they may have, are disqualified from being called pilsners on the grounds of a general lack of hop assertiveness and/or too light a body, sometimes caused deliberately by the use of rice in the mash.

Warsteiner

Brewer	Warsteiner
Strength (ABV)	4.8%
Description	Light aroma. Slightly malt-accented flavour with a touch of bitterness.

Smoked Beers

The German word *rauch* means 'smoked'. Most beers today are brewed from barley that has been dried in a kiln sealed from the source of heat. Before such sophisticated methods were adopted, the barley must have been kilned by coming into direct contact with fire, producing grains of malt that would impart a smoky flavour.

In Northern Bavaria, the town of Bamberg has long been associated with smoked beers. The most prestigious brew is Aecht Schlenkerla Rauchbier, labelled a Märzen. Beechwood from the forests nearby fuels the fire that dries the barley, and the effects of the smoke are very evident in the finished product. Only smoked malt is used in brewing the beer, which is bottom-fermented to a strength of 4.8% ABV.

The Kaiserdom beers from Bürgerbräu include a rauchbier. Though called *Lagerbier* (a rare example of Germans using the word as the British do), the beer from Spezial of that name is a rauchbier, as is their stronger Märzen. In France, the Adelscott beers from the Adelshoffen brewery near Strasburg are made with malt smoked over peat, whisky-style. Across the Atlantic, the Alaskan Brewing Company produce a smoked porter.

A variation, called Rauchenfels Steinbier and originally from Neustadt to the north of Bamberg but now brewed further south in Altenmünster, involves brewing the beer with the help of very hot stones, specially imported from Austria to be heated over beechwood. These are added to the copper boil and, when cool, are then placed in the tanks where the beer matures. The stones pick up various accretions from the boil that remain during the conditioning period, so their impact upon the final taste has a double edge.

Aecht Schlenkerla Rauchbier

Brewery	Schlenkerla
Strength (ABV)	4.8%
Description	Red-brown colour. Overpowering aroma of kippers that, in a more balanced and malty form, becomes embedded in the flavour.

Special Lagers

Those listed here include the internationally available pale lagers that may not fit a particular category but stand out for one reason or another. Some are quite powerful, such as the Carlsberg duo, Elephant Beer (7.1% ABV) and Special (8.5% ABV), neither of them aimed at the draught or canned market that Carlsberg attracts with its usual licensed brews. Various premium lagers sold in swing-top bottles are headed by Grolsch from the

Carlsberg Elephant
(Denmark) • 7.2% ABV

Grolsch (Netherlands)
• 5.0% ABV

Netherlands, with its Premium at 5.0% ABV. Of the mass-produced draught lagers, the Belgian-originated Stella Artois deserves mention as the first to spread itself widely at premium strength.

From the Czech Republic, Budweiser Budvar doesn't quite conform to the pilsener style, being more amber then golden, even softer in texture and less bitter, but with a sweetness that captivates rather than cloys. Another near-pilsener, growing in availability beyond its North American base, is Samuel Adams Boston Lager.

Stella Artois
(Belgium) • 5.2% ABV

Samuel Adams Boston Lager
(USA) • 4.8% ABV

107

Budweiser Budvar

Brewery	Budejovice
Strength (ABV)	5.0%
Description	Light amber colour. Beautifully balanced malt-hop flavour, dominated by very soft texture.

Jever Pils

Brewery	Jever
Strength (ABV)	4.9%
Description	Bitter-citric aroma. Full, slightly oily texture, very strong bitter taste.

A handful of German pilseners far exceed the Czech original in bitterness, the most widely accessible being Jever from the town of that name near Hamburg, probably the most bitter lager in the world. Several hundred miles to the east, Singha lager is an exceptionally bitter and flavoursome product from the Thai brewery, one of many examples of German brewing influence in that part of Asia.

Vienna Lagers

The importance of Vienna in the evolution of lagers goes back to the mid-1800s and Anton Dreher, whose style of lager was adopted by brewers in Munich when they wanted something new for the Oktoberfest. Dreher had created a bottom-fermented beer that was soft in texture, smooth and malty, with a colour that set it aside from the common run – bronze or reddish, rather than the dark lagers that preceded the golden pilsener age.

Until recently, there was little recognition of this in Vienna itself – surprising until you remember how often styles of beer are threatened by the dictates of fashion. As a kind of halfway house between dark and pale, these lagers must have been squeezed out.

Dos Equis XX (Mexico) • 4.8% ABV

Beer connoisseur Michael Jackson has noted how, after writing learnedly on this subject not that long ago, he was accused by some Austrians of making it up!

Just as porters could be found in far-flung lands after they had vanished from their birthplace in the UK, so did lagers in the Vienna style take root in Mexico – once under Austrian rule – with such brands as Dos Equis and Negra Modelo. The style also survives as a speciality in several winter beers from Scandinavian countries and, as usual, there are intriguing, individualised examples from the newer breed of brewers in the USA.

A common ingredient is amber malt, which Jackson mentions is sometimes referred to in the trade as 'Vienna malt': as another kind of halfway house between the contrasting colouring malts, amber declined in use but is itself enjoying a revival, mainly among ale brewers.

Negra Modelo

Brewery	Modelo
Strength (ABV)	5.3%
Description	Reddish-brown colour. Very smooth, soft texture to go with underlying taste of malt.

ALES & BITTERS
Abbey Ales

The production of beers that resemble, in varying degrees, those brewed in monasteries has been spread widely. Agreements between a brewer of abbey beers and an actual abbey can vary. Close relationships exist today between, for example, the Benedictine abbey at Affligem and the De Smedt brewery nearby, and between the Floreffe abbey near Namur and the Lefèbvre brewery, some 60 kilometres to the north-west. In both cases, beers under the abbey name are produced under licence.

Two of the more widely available abbey beers emanate from Belgium's biggest brewers. The abbeys of Leffe and Grimbergen have beers brewed by, respectively, Interbrew and Alken-Maes, whose total operations put both among the top ten brewing companies worldwide. Ename (from Roman), Witkap (from Slaghmuylder) and Bornem (from van Steenberghe) are among those appearing under the Dubbel and Tripel banners.

Abbey beers aim to reproduce the full-tasting, heavily flavoured characteristics associated with the Chimays and the Rocheforts. However, the similarity does not necessarily extend, say, to the beers re-fermenting in the bottle (though Ename, Maredsous, Witkap and others do so), or to the complexity of the

Grimbergen Tripel

Brewery	Alken-Maes
Strength (ABV)	9.0%
Description	Golden-amber colour.
	Faint pear-almond aroma.
	Full texture, with a heavy sweet-nutty flavour the sweetness blending with the bitter-almond finish

brewing process. Sometimes, there is no abbey link at all, beyond the intention and/or the name of the beer. The style, if one may so describe something that exists as much by association as anything else, has even been taken up in the USA.

An analogy with classic wines can be made. Anyone wanting a well-packaged, readily drinkable and affordable version of a famous brand has a wide choice: however, there is no substitute for a real Trappist ale.

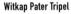

Witkap Pater Tripel

Brewery	Slaghmuylder
Strength (ABV)	7.5%
Description	Yellow colour. Wheaty, slightly smoked flavour that develops a bitter aftertaste.

American Ale

All the beers developed over the centuries by European brewers have their counterparts in the USA. Before the recent revival, by far the most common were the bottom-fermented beers inspired by the German heritage of the Anheusers, Strohs and Pabsts.

These still dominate today, but the growth of the microbrewery movement has led to the products of the UK and Belgium – the principal ale-brewing countries – being emulated more widely. Even the biggest US brewers, such as Miller, are now producing ales that are intended to taste of something.

Little Kings Cream Ale (USA) • 5.0% ABV

The freedom with which Americans interpret traditional styles is especially evident where ales are concerned, notably in the flavour imparted by the highly potent and aromatic American hops. It could have influenced the pale ale from the

St Stan's Red Sky Ale

Brewery	St. Stan's
Strength (ABV)	5.9%
Description	Pale colour. Strong aroma of herbs. Citric, decidedly hoppy flavour that becomes sharp and dry in the finish.

highly-regarded Sierra Nevada brewery, which also hits you with the citrusy scent from Cascade hops while offering more complex flavours when swallowed. A different tradition is followed by St Stan's brewery, which draws inspiration from the top-fermenting *altbiers* of Düsseldorf. Most ales from the newer brigade tend to various degrees of hoppiness: as mentioned in the section on IPA (see p. 137), American examples of such beers taste extremely bitter.

The designation 'cream ale' has been applied to a style of American ale that predates the current revival. The name implies a smoothness of texture, and these beers are readily drinkable as well as being light in colour and not over-strong.

Apart from cream ales, and similar survivals such as Ballantine's and Rainier's ales, not many beers from the previous resurgence in American brewing were commonly available. But now the American influence is in turn heading east as more of their hops cross the Atlantic and several of the beers produced by, in particular, the newer UK microbrewers are taking on their characteristics.

Sierra Nevada Pale

Brewery	Sierra Nevada
Strength (ABV)	5.3%
Description	Light amber colour. Powerful citric aroma, leading to a smoothly rounded bitter-malt taste

Barley Wine

Wine comes from the grape and beer from malted barley, so you might call the name a contradiction in terms. There is no agreement as to the origins of this name, but it does seem appropriate: the alcoholic strength approaches that of a wines and the taste is often vinous, though closer to port or sherry than to a glass of Burgundy (let alone Moselle).

Barley wines are top-fermenting ales of at least 6.5% ABV that tend towards darkish colours, from amber-

red to deep brown. There is some overlap with old ales, especially in the names of such beers as Robinson's Old Tom, Marston's Owd Roger, Young's Old Nick and, from the USA, Anchor's Old Foghorn,

Robinson's Old Tom

Brewery	Robinson
Strength (ABV)	8.5%
Description	Ruby brown colour.
	Fruity, slightly vinous aroma.
	Full, rich, malt-molasses flavour, with
	bitterness coming through in the finish.

all of which should arguably be classified as barley wines because of their strength and the way they are marketed. They receive extra conditioning, while the brewer's art comes in modifying the sweetness inherent in beers brewed to a high original gravity, by putting in plenty of hops and/or by fermenting out the beer thoroughly.

While some are also sold on draught over the pub counter, the usual container is a small bottle, rarely bigger than 275 ml and sometimes in the nip-sized 180 ml – a third of a pint – the trend recently has been

upwards, but Whitbread's Gold Label still comes in nips. This is the most widely available of barley wines and unambiguously marketed as such; the same applies to a remarkable American new-comer, Sierra Nevada's Big Foot Barley Wine (around 12.0% ABV).

Gold Label (UK)

Brewery	Whitbread
Strength (ABV)	10.9%
Description	Amber colour. Slightly fruity aroma. Bitter on the palate, with a powerful taste of almonds that lingers

Belgian Brown Ale

About 70 kilometres due west of Brussels, the town of Oudenaarde contains Liefmans brewery. The most famous of all Belgian brown ales are still produced here, even if the mashing and boiling takes place in the nearby Riva brewery in Dentergem, owners of Liefman's for the past few years. After the brew, using specially adapted water and given a very long boil, the

Goudenband

Brewery	Liefmans
Strength (ABV)	8.0%
Description	Brown-red colour.
	Faint nutty-almond aroma.
	Full texture, bitter-sweet, slightly sour palette with underlying maltiness.
	Bitter-sweet finish.

fermentation is carried out at Oudenaarde with the help of the Liefman yeast. After a week in traditional open squares, the beer conditions for several months.

Unlike the brown ales found in the UK, these are sharp, slightly sour in taste and, unsurprisingly, form the basis of fruit beers that compare with the lambic krieks and frambozens. Blending is also a characteristic of these top-fermented beers: Liefmans Oud Broun, which conditions for at least a month, is mixed with a more mature version. Thus blended, the beer re-ferments in the bottle for three months before being put on sale as Goudenband.

Other notable brown ales of this type come from Oudenaarde's Clarysse brewery and from Roman, a few miles east.

Belgian Pale Ale

Apart from strong ales, of which Duvel is the front runner, and beers that fall into the Trappist or abbey category, Belgium also produces a handful of pale ales at a lower strength. Those most widely available tend to have a less fruity aroma and be slightly darker in colour, while there are more hints of sourness in the taste – the same applies when comparing them with the majority of British ales of premium strength and above.

The De Koninck brewery of Antwerp is particularly celebrated for a pale ale, served in all the local bars in

Palm Speciale

Brewery	Palm
Strength (ABV)	5.0%
Description	Light brown colour. Tart aroma. Soft texture, malty, with bitter overtones.

the traditional tall-stemmed glass known as a *bolleke*. From the Palm brewery in the village of Steenhuffel, Palm Speciale is the big seller, a quarter of production exported to Holland and elsewhere. Straffe Hendrik's beer of 5.4% ABV is paler and gives off more of a fruity-hoppy aroma. The same applies to ales from breweries in Wallonia, such as La Binchoise, Abbaye Des Rocs and Dupont.

De Koninck

Brewery	De Koninck
Strength (ABV)	5.0%
Description	Copper-bronze colour. Malty, slightly sharp taste, with citric hoppiness.

Belgian Red Ale

A Belgian classic, the style is associated above all with the Rodenbach brewery in Roeselare, south of Bruges. Their beers are top-fermented and matured in oak vats – well over 200, in sizesup to 60,000 litres (13,200 gallons) capacity – for up to two years, the aged wood helping to impart the characteristic sourness as well as contributing to the deep red colour.

Hops for these ales are selected for their preservative qualities and not for their contribution to the final taste. Yet another similarity with the

Rodenbach

Brewery	Rodenbach
Strength (ABV)	5.0%
Description	Red-brown colour.
	Sharp and sour aroma. Smooth texture, sour palate that becomes refreshing and thirst-quenching.

production of lambics comes in the blending of young and old beers, matured for respectively 6 weeks and 18–24 months respectively to produce the standard Rodenbach (5.0% ABV). The older beer is also sold on its own under the name of Rodenbach Grand Cru. Both beers are pasteurized before leaving the brewery, as is Alexander, a version of the Grand Cru with cherries.

Two breweries to the east of Roeselare produce red ales of similar style in Bacchus, from Van Honsebrouck, and Petrus from Bavik-De Brabandere. Often compared to Rodenbach, Strong Suffolk from the UK's Greene King is also a blend of brews matured for different periods in wooden casks. More recently in Holland, the Gulpener brewery has re-introduced a beer, called Mestreechs Aajt, that ferments with wild yeast, conditions in wood for a year and is then blended with a conventional lager.

Belgian Strong Ale

Once mainly a pilsener brewery, Moortgat in Breendonk started to change direction in the 1920s when the son of the founder came to Britain to learn about brewing ale. However, the resulting beer, which he eventually named Duvel 'devil' on the grounds that 'the Devil is in me after 2-3 glasses', did not really take off until the 1970s. Since then, it has become Moortgat's leading brand.

All bottle-conditioned, it goes through a complex process before being passed fit for drinking. Glucose is added to the beer before fermentation, after which it conditions for three weeks. With a fresh dose of yeast, the beer then re-ferments in the bottle for at least ten days in a

Lucifer (Belgium)
• 8.0% ABV

warm cellar before finally being stored under cooler temperatures awaiting collection. The finished article is full-bodied, packed with flavour and surprisingly bitter for a beer of more than 8.5% ABV. Duvel changes in character over a period of about three years. Between six months and year after bottling, the levels of bitterness, aroma and carbonation in the beer reach a happy equilibrium. From then, the flavour develops in weird and wonderful ways as the fizz and aroma decline further.

Following the success of Duvel, other breweries joined the market for strong beers, pale or golden in colour. Riva's Lucifer, Alken-Maes's Judas and Hoegaarden's Grand Cru are among the leading brands. In a class of its own is Bush, at 12.0% ABV.

Mechelson Bruyen (Belgium)
•6.0% ABV

From an equal range of strong brown ales (not to be confused with the sour Liefmans type), the most prestigious is Gouden Carolus from the Anker brewery in Mechelen, where such beers have been brewed for centuries. At 7.5% ABV and with a

Gouden Carolus

Brewery	Het Anker
Strength (ABV)	7.5%
Description	Deep brown colour. Heavy vinous taste, rich, fruity and warming, remains all the way to the finish.

deep, reddish-brown colour, it drinks fully up to its strength, a ripe, toffeeish aroma leading to a powerfully throat-warming taste. A weaker beer from Anker, Mechelsen Bruyen, is lighter in colour and has a nutty flavour resembling a British brown ale.

A close relationship between beer and the glass from which you drink it characterizes the Belgian scene, where individually designed glasses for the different beers adds to the fun of going to the bar or cafe. One of the most distinctive, a kind of test tube or miniature yard of ale that comes with its own wooden stand, belongs to Pauwel's Kwak, a lightish-coloured brown ale that, at 8.5% ABV, ranks among the strongest of its kind.

Duvel

Brewery	Moortgat
Strength (ABV)	8.5%
Description	Golden colour. Fruity (pear) aroma. Light texture and rounded, quite bitter flavour that lingers in the aftertaste.

Bière de Garde

The northernmost part of France shares with French-speaking Belgium, just across the border, the presence of smallish brewers. These are often described as 'artisanal', a reminder that this was an area of mines and factories where beer did its bit to lubricate the industrial process. Beer from most of the survivors, plus that from a handful of new arrivals, can be compared to the classier Belgian products. A term applied to some of these is Bière de Garde, because they were traditionally unfiltered and designed to mature further in the bottle when laid down in the cellar.

Few meet that criterion today, but the beers still retain an identity. By tradition, they were top-fermented ales; some breweries compromise today by using a lager-type yeast but ferment at a temperature of 15 °C/60 °F – halfway between lager and

Jenlain

Brewery	Duyck
Strength (ABV)	6.5%
Description	Light-red colour. Sharp aroma. Full-bodied, slightly tart with bitter-sweet undertones in the finish.

ale. From the Duyck brewery near Valenciennes, Jenlain is the best-known internationally, light brown in colour and, characteristically, drinking up to its strength of 6.5% ABV. Also increasingly available outside the area are beers from the Benifontaine brewery of Castelain, founded in 1926 but taken over by the Castelain family forty years later and completely renovated. Beers marketed under the Ch'ti trademark include Blonde, Brune and Ambrée.

La Choulette is over a hundred years old and brews San Culottes and the darker La Choulette at a farmhouse in Hordain. Other brewers include St. Sylvestre with Trois Monts, and Annoeullin with Pastor Ale.

Whatever the colour, the beers are strong and full-tasting, with a complexity of flavours developing out of a spicy sweetness. The strengths range from 6.0% ABV (Ch'ti Ambrée) to 8.5% ABV (Trois Monts).

Ch'ti

Brewery	Castelain
Strength (ABV)	6.5%
Description	Pale colour. Fruity aroma, leading to full, clean, slightly wheaty taste with a touch of bitterness.

Bitter

The British love of going out to drink beer in bulk encourages brewers to keep the strength down. As the average alcohol content of beer has dropped steadily for decades – though it may be levelling out or even rising as premium beers and those brewed for special occasions take a higher share of the draught beer market – nowadays ordinary pub bitter (or lager) generally weighs in at under 4.0% ABV.

As a descriptive term, 'bitter' does not always fit the bill. It should best be contrasted with 'mild', which usually has a low hop rate and a sweeter taste. Bitters vary in colour from light brown to golden. The more bitter bitters are found in South-East England and, in particular, parts of Lancashire and Yorkshire.

Holt's Bitter

Brewery	Joseph Holt
Strength (ABV)	4.0%
Description	Medium-bronze colour. Sharp, malty flavour that soon gives way to a pronounced and lasting bitterness.

Beers of this strength are not expected to make much of a commercial impact in bottled form. Some pubs in some parts of the country still do a reasonable trade in mixed draught/bottled beers. The 'light' component of a 'light and bitter' may be the draught bitter itself processed in bottled form, or possibly a similar but weaker beer.

As the demand for such mixtures falls, the smaller brewers are less likely to produce their own bottled lights or bitters and stock those from other breweries. There has been a trend towards brewing bottled light ales centrally, where the identical beer is given different labels appropriate to the breweries owning the pubs in which it will be sold.

Ridley's IPA

Brewery	TD Ridley
Strength (ABV)	3.5%
Description	Copper coloured. Well-balanced malty-bitter flavour backed by a tangy edge.

Brown Ale

The bottled counterpart to mild, brown ales were once widely available in pubs, either for drinking on their own or as part of a mixture. In recent years, the 'brown-bitters' and 'brown and milds' have all but disappeared. As happened to light ales in the UK, only more so, bottles of brown now come from a mere handful of breweries. They are low in alcohol and in hop rate, the taste sweet with a hint of toast.

Among the few survivors is Mann's Brown Ale, kept on by the former Watney group (which took over Mann's brewery at some point in their rise to national status) and most recently transferred to the now-independent Usher's brewery, who brew it under contract. One of the less foreseeable successes of the

Pete's Wicked Ale (USA) • 5.1% ABV

US revival has been Brooklyn Brown Ale. Although at 6.0% ABV this is much stronger than any similar British product, it captures all of the traditional taste and enhances it through a judicious use of hops. Another American product enjoying even wider currency is Pete's Wicked Ale, red-brown in colour and untraditionally hoppy.

But for many people, 'brown ale' means a different

Double Maxim (UK)
• 4.7% ABV

Samuel Smith's
Nut Brown Ale
(UK)• 5.0% ABV

product – one that has never gone away. Bottles of Newcastle Brown Ale are drunk throughout the world, and such other prominent North-East

England breweries as Vaux, with Double Maxim, and Samuel Smith, with Nut Brown Ale, produce comparable brands. Intended to be consumed by themselves rather than as part of a mix, these are stronger than the Mann's type, more amber-red than brown and have a smooth, slightly oily texture with a sharpish aftertaste.

Newcastle Brown Ale

Brewery	Scottish-Courage
Strength (ABV)	4.7%
Description	Bronze-red colour. Sharp malty flavour, with bitter-sweetness that lingers.

Brooklyn Brown Ale

Brewery	Brooklyn
Strength (ABV)	6.0%
Description	Deep red colour. Fruity aroma. Smooth texture, light hoppy taste with hint of chocolate.

German Ale

Despite a reputation built around bottom-fermented beers, Germany also brews ales (quite apart from its top-fermenting wheat beers). These tend to be localized, to the extent that the two best-known examples are associated with a particular city.

The so-called *altbiers* of Düsseldorf are brewed in a similar fashion to the British ales, but then given the lager treatment by being left for a few weeks to condition in tanks under cold temperatures. As a result the finished article, dark in colour, tends to develop a texture more full than a British ale of comparable strength and to have a pronounced malt flavour, though bitterness definitely comes through. Altbiers are available on draught in Düsseldorf, and some of

Schlösser Alt

Brewery	Schlösser
Strength (ABV)	4.8%
Description	Red-brown colour.
	Slight citric-pear aroma.
	Dry, full-flavoured, bitter more than sweet but very well balanced.

the best examples are brewed on the premises.

Not far away, Cologne turns out Kölschbier. By law, that name cannot be used for beer brewed anywhere else, which explains why most kölschbiers do not travel far. The brewing and conditioning process resembles that of the altbiers, apart from wheat being sometimes added to the mash, but the result is very different: a pale-coloured, light-textured, fruity-flavoured beer with a hint of hops. Again, it is best drunk in a brewpub.

A recent innovation from the Maisel brewery in Bayreuth is Dampfbier, a russet-coloured beer of 4.9% ABV, with a sparkling character and light bitterness resembling an English ale.

Früh Kölsch

Brewery	Cölner Hofbräu Früh
Strength (ABV)	4.8%
Description	Golden colour. Apple-pear aroma. Very soft texture, rounded, quite fruity, slight bitterness in the finish.

India Pale Ale

Because its water was especially suited to making pale ales, the town of Burton upon Trent supplied most of the beer shipped to India for the benefit of troops fighting for their corner of the British Empire. In order to reach the troops in a drinkable form after a long journey involving sea travel and variable temperatures, India Pale Ales were brewed with an abundance of hops and to a high gravity. By the time they were drunk, the beers had mellowed.

Fuggles Imperial (UK)
• 5.5% ABV

Several British draught beers that had progressively less to do with the Indian tradition, apart from colour, continued to use the name. Once the revived interest in beer led to research into how those IPAs were brewed, something of a revival took place, in the draught as well as in the speciality bottled market.

This occurred on both sides of the Atlantic, and there is an interesting diversity of approach. On the whole, the newer British IPAs are between 4.0% and 5.0% ABV and bitter. In the USA, the tendency has been to make IPAs very strong and very bitter, reflecting how they probably would have tasted when they left the brewery rather than when they ended up in India.

One of the UK's stronger and more bitter examples, Fuggles Imperial IPA at 5.5% ABV, became the first of Whitbread's speciality draught beers brewed with just one hop variety (in this case, the Fuggle) to become part of the company's regular portfolio. The more successful commercially of the newer breed include Marston's India Export Pale Ale, appropriately from Burton upon Trent, and Deuchars IPA from Edinburgh's Caledonian brewery, where the tang of hops blends with the typically full, slightly sweet Scottish flavour.

King & Barnes IPA (UK)
• 5.0% ABV

Deuchars IPA

Brewery	Caledonian
Strength (ABV)	4.4%
Description	Light amber colour. Firm texture, underlying maltiness, with citric tang and hops coming through in the finish.

Marston's India Export Pale Ale

Brewer	Marston, Thompson & Evershed
Strength (ABV)	5.5%
Description	Amber colour. Light pear-apple aroma. Very soft, slightly oily texture, with a bitterness that grows pronounced in the finish.

Irish Red Ale

Until recently, the only Irish ales making a splash outside Ireland were the stouts. In the UK, at least, this has begun to change with the spread of so-called nitrokegs. Caffreys from Bass's Belfast brewery, followed by Kilkenny from a Guinness-owned brewery in the Republic of Ireland are the front-runners, joined by an increasing number of imitations from national and regional British breweries, for whom the method of dispense often counts for more than colour or flavour.

Caffreys (Ireland)
• 4.8% ABV

Light-red coloured, strongish, malt-flavoured beers represent an Irish tradition and, before the sudden upsurge, the brand most widely available went under the name of George Killian. The Lett brewery in County Wexford shut down in the 1960s, but one of the family, George Killian Lett, gave Pelforth in France (now part of Heineken) and the US Coors brewery the licence to brew the beer. Sold in bottles, the Pelforth brew is particularly substantial, with a strength of 6.5% ABV.

As for the products on sale as draught beers in the UK, the smooth texture imparted by nitrogen, which is less biting than carbon dioxide, and the cooler-than-ale temperatures prevail over any noticeable flavour. Some of the regional products are nitrokeg versions of an existing ale; in a comparison, it is noticeable how much of the taste is lost, probably as much from cooling as from being conditioned at the brewery.

Kilkenny's Irish Beer

Brewery	Guinness
Strength (ABV)	5.0%
Description	Bronze-red colour. Creamy, slightly oily texture, bitter-sweet flavour, hint of walnuts.

Mild

Once the best-selling draught beer in the UK, mild has all but disappeared from many localities. Efforts to preserve it have had some success, in that a specialist pub or two in most areas will stock a mild, often in the form of a changing guest beer.

Whatever it might have been in the past, mild today is a sweetish beer, often 3.5% ABV or below and usually darkish in colour. It remains popular in the West Midlands, notably as the key product of two substantial firms. One of the biggest regional brewers,

Banks's Mild

Brewery	Wolverhampton & Dudley
Strength (ABV)	3.5%
Description	Light brown colour. Smooth texture, well-balanced, fruity flavour, slightly sweet.

Wolverhampton & Dudley, produce Banks's Mild in Wolverhampton. The Highgate & Walsall brewery, which recently gained its independence from Bass, for many years produced nothing but Highgate Mild. National brands aimed at the West Midlands include Bass's M&B Mild from Birmingham and Ansell's Mild, once of Birmingham but currently brewed some distance away at Burton upon Trent.

Deep in the West Midlands, the Sarah Hughes micro brewery brews a Dark Ruby Mild at 6.0% ABV. The strength makes it truly exceptional for a mild today. An example of the light-coloured milds more traditional to the south of England is McMullen's AK. In Scotland, the equivalent product to mild may be called 60/-. Brain's Dark from Cardiff is widely available in its area.

Kimberley Best Mild (UK)
• 3.1% ABV

Old Ale

These traditional UK products are dark in colour and full-tasting. Beyond that, they may differ from each other notably in strength, from a lower base of around 4.0% ABV to 6.0%, and above. With some brewers, the cut-off point between old ales and barley wines is hard to determine.

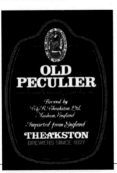

As a heavy, warming drink, old ales are often confined to the winter months, at least in draught form – a trend that grows as many brewers introduce a wider range of seasonal beers. They should be brewed using

Theakston's Old Peculier

Brewery	Scottish-Courage
Strength (ABV)	5.6%
Description	Dark-brown colour.
	Fruity aroma, slightly roasted.
	Full texture, bitter-chocolate with hint of coffee.
	Slightly hoppy aftertaste.

enough roasted malt to impart a sweetish flavour, perhaps suggesting toffee-molasses overtones, and without the more pronounced bitterness you get from stouts or even from porters. Some firms use the term 'old' as a simple alternative to mild or bitter: Brakspear's Old, Harvey's Old, Adnam's Old and so on.

Others may incorporate the term as part of a more elaborate title, in the manner of Theakston's Old Peculier. A seasonal beer such as Young's long-standing Winter Warmer is an old in all but name.

Adnam's Old Ale

Brewery	Adnams
Strength (ABV)	4.1%
Description	Dark-brown colour. Round, fruity aroma. Creamy texture, warming roast-malt flavour leading to a bitter-sweet finish.

Pale Ale

This is included as a separate section in order to highlight a number of special beers. In fact, many bitters and all beers listed under 'India Pale Ale'(see p.137) could be featured under this heading.

First brewed in the days when most bottled beers contained sediment and underwent some form of secondary fermentation, Worthington White Shield is the

King & Barnes Pale Ale (UK)
• 3.5% ABV

only survivor of its kind, especially if you exclude beers that are strong and dark. To keep going, it has indeed led a nomadic existence. Worthington itself was taken over by Bass, also of Burton upon Trent, when it became simply a matter of transferring the brewing down the road. But firms with large-scale plants often have logistic problems in meeting the demands of a small and specialist market, and White Shield has since been moved twice within the Bass empire, and is now brewed under contract in Sussex by King & Barnes.

Occasionally given a splash of publicity and sustained by the enthusiasm of a handful of

Worthington White Shield

Brewery	Bass
Strength (ABV)	5.6%
Description	Amber-red colour. Fruity orange-like aroma, with malty-nutty flavour, quite dry and with underlying bitterness.

discerning Bass employees, the beer is brewed conventionally until the end, when it is filtered, re-seeded (with a different yeast) and left to condition for three weeks in the bottle. It is best drunk within 3–18 months, during which time the character evolves without losing a slightly oily dryness.

Across the world, Cooper's in Adelaide is likewise a survivor, in this case the only long-established Australian brewery to weather the craze for mass-produced cans of lager. Cooper's Sparkling Ale is top-fermented, filtered and then given back a small amount of the unfiltered wort to help it condition in the bottle.

Sparkling Ale

Brewery	Cooper's
Strength (ABV)	5.8%
Description	Yellow-golden colour. Light nutty aroma. Soft texture and fruity flavour with slight hoppiness in background live up to the beer's name.

Saisons

Beers brewed for a particular time of year have never gone away. The tradition of producing strong beers for the cold winter months of countries in the northern hemisphere, not least to be consumed over Christmas, has been supplemented by other seasonal endeavours, some with the aim of promoting the public's awareness of beer and breweries.

Silly Saison (Belgium)
• 5.0% ABV

Saisons from the French-speaking areas of Belgium, notably the province of Hainault, are survivors of a tradition when the climate laid down when one could brew. Most common were the March saisons, brewed to last over the summer months when brewing was impossible. These top-fermenting beers, often intended to be consumed by farm workers, contained sufficient alcohol (about 5.0–6.0% ABV) and a heavy dose of hops to help them survive a long time and withstand the hot temperatures. Appropriately for a beer meant to keep, they underwent a secondary fermentation in the cask, as they still do in the bottle in some cases. Some are brewed with spices in addition to hops.

For beers not intended to be excessively strong, they

have the solid mouthfeel characteristic of a beer whi
has not fully fermented. Today, they tend towards a de
yellow colour, and a sweet/sour taste that might co
from mixing old and young beers in the conditioni
tank, with candy sugar added to stimulate activity.

The Dupont brewery of Hainaut is renowned especia
for the much-admired Vieille Provision (6.5% AB
Other saisons froom Wallonia include Lefèbvre's 19
Saison, Du Bocq's Saison Regal and the Saison Silly fro
Silly (the brewery of the town of that name that happily jo
in the laughter it draws from English-speaking visitors).

Saison Regal

Brewery	Du Bocq
Strength (ABV)	6.0%
Description	Amber-copper colour. Strong pear-apple aroma. Creamy texture, sour-sweet, malty flavour with a ight tang of hops. Fruity aftertaste.

Scotch Ale

There is a tradition in Scotland of producing slightly sweet, full-flavoured, malty ales. This applies right across the board. Such descriptions as 'mild' and 'bitter' were rarely used: instead, they devised a system that related the strength of the beer to the predecimalized excise duty payable, namely 60/-, 70/- and 80/-, with the first a dark counterpart to the English mild and the last a premium ale.

Some breweries, including Edinburgh's Caledonian Brewery that regained its independence a few years ago and still relies on a plant including direct-fired coppers, deliberately leave part of the finished beer

Caledonian 80/- (UK)
• 4.2% ABV

unfermented. This contributes to both the fullness of texture and the rounded taste. Among the older-established breweries, similar qualities are found in the beers of Belhaven of Dunbar, in those from the giant Scottish-Courage brewery in Edinburgh and

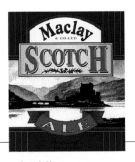

Scotch Ale

Brewery	Maclay
Strength (ABV)	5.0%
Description	Medium-amber colour. Slightly nutty aroma. Full, smooth, malty flavour, with a nutty-sweet undertone and a dry-bitter finish.

those of Maclay's of Alloa, though the latter lean perhaps more towards an English sharpness. The popularity has spread to Belgium, where Gordon's Scotch Ale is imported after being brewed in Edinburgh by Scottish-Courage.

St Andrew's Ale

Brewery	Belhaven
Strength (ABV)	4.6%
Description	Red-brown colour. Nutty-apple aroma. Very malty, full-tasting, with a hint of roasted nuts. Bitter-sweet aftertaste.

Special Bitter

With the UK special (or premium) bitters, cross-fertilization may take place between draught and bottled. Some, perhaps a majority, of bottled brands have been given a separate identity and the word 'bitter' is seldom incorporated in the logo. These are ales, mostly pale rather than dark and mostly between 4.0% and 5.0% ABV, but otherwise with few standardized characteristics.

Landlord

Brewery	Timothy Taylor
Strength (ABV)	4.3%
Description	Pale-copper colour. Full texture, with characteristically hoppy, citric, slightly musty flavour and a bitter aftertaste.

Some of the new small firms aim for a section of the market where novelty takes precedence. The rest, including national and the surviving regional brewers, produce regular specials on draught to complement

6X

Brewery	Wadworth
Strength (ABV)	4.3%
Description	Copper-brown colour. Full texture, malty with undertones of hop bitterness that lead to a bitter finish.

their ordinary bitters. Specials will usually have a fuller mouthfeel, helped by the extra alcohol, and taste less dry and more sweet, though sometimes an underlying bitterness comes through at the end. In most cases, the colour will also be darker.

Complementing differences between ordinary bitters and specials, the variations among specials themselves in general run parallel to those affecting the bitters: sharper in the South-East (Young's Special and Harvey's Tom Paine); maltier in the South-West (Wadworth's 6X); sweeter in the Midlands (Batham's

Tom Paine

Brewery	Harvey
Strength (ABV)	5.5%
Description	Yellow-bronze colour. Full texture, dominated by hop flavours, mainly fruity with a rounded bitterness.

Bitter and Holden's Special), then becoming hoppier as you go north until you reach the sweeter, full-tasting premium beers of Scotland.

The musty fruitiness of Taylor's Landlord from Keighley has been emulated by newer Yorkshire brewers. Bateman's beers from Lincolnshire, notably their XXXB at 4.8% ABV, have a pronounced flowery taste.

Old Speckled Hen

Brewery	Morland
Strength (ABV)	5.2%
Description	Light tawny colour. Malty flavour, but dry and underpinned by distinctive almond-tinged tang of hop bitterness.

Steam Beer

Although 'steam' has been used in the names of other beers, most drinkers link it automatically with the Anchor brewery of San Francisco, one of the great survivors, along with its Steam Beer. Nobody knows exactly who invented the term. The theory commonly accepted is that 'steam' represented the excessive build-up of carbon dioxide, caused by the beer fermenting in the shallow vessels used by local

Anchor Steam Beer

Brewery	Anchor
Strength (ABV)	5.0%
Description	Light brown colour. Fruity aroma. Full texture, malty with bitter and vinous undertones that prevail in the aftertaste.

breweries that were not temperature-controlled but just cooled by the San Francisco air. When a cask was eventually tapped, the escaping gas made a noise that reminded listeners of the hissing sound emanating from steam engines.

Making steam beer something of a lager-ale hybrid, the yeast inserted in these unrefrigerated shallow vessels is of the bottom-fermenting kind. The refrigerated tanks in which the beer then conditions are pressurized to withstand the residual gas, and bags containing whole hops are inserted to dry-hop the beer. At the end, any yeast remaining is taken out by centrifuge and the beer is pasteurized by a flash hot-and-cold system that allows the beer to retain enough of its own gas to live on.

Strong Ales

Somewhere between the premium/special bitters and the barley wines, these are beers wholly, or most widely, available in bottled form and of more than 5.0% ABV in strength. In the UK, they may be survivors of the days before the market for bottled beer all but disappeared, being kept going largely as flagship products and to satisfy a handful of connoisseurs.

Greene King's St. Edmunds Ale, Shepherd Neame's Bishop's Finger and Sneck Lifter from Jennings are among those from the older-established brewers, while Golden Hill's Exmoor Gold, Hop Back's Summer Lightning, Wychwood's Hobgoblin and Black Sheep's Riggwelter Ale are just a handful from the new small breweries available in bottled form. Fuller's excellent ESB is an example of a long-standing draught beer that has been bottled, the gravity increased (from 5.6% to 6.0% ABV) in order to compensate for any flavour lost by filtering and pasteurization.

Bishop's Finger (UK) • 5.4% ABV

Generally yellow-amber in colour, the beers have a high malt content and a strong hoppy taste, fruity rather than bitter, with a full body that comes from extra conditioning, often at both warm and cold temperatures. Young's Special London Ale (previously known as Strong Export) conditions for a minimum of six weeks, the last four of them in cold storage. During this period, it is heavily dry-hopped with pellets of Golding aromatic hops, which are very noticeable in the final taste.

Norman's Conquest (UK)
• 7% ABV

Young's Special London Ale was almost certainly an inspiration for Anchor's Liberty Ale from San Francisco, first brewed in 1975 to celebrate the bicentenary of Paul Revere's ride. Intended as a one-off beer, it was clearly too good to jettison and, having evolved over the years, became part of Anchor's regular portfolio in 1984. Brewed entirely from pale malt, it has a very powerful citrus aroma that comes from Cascade hops. The taste, though, has a more mellow, Golding-type fruitiness, close to that of a British ale: as with Young's ale, dry-hopping plays an important part, in this case by hops enclosed in perforated containers being added to the maturation tank. The contrast between what you smell and how the beer tastes makes Liberty Ale a classic, one that in turn has inspired several newer American breweries.

Special London Ale

Brewery	Young
Strength (ABV)	6.4%
Description	Amber colour. Light citric aroma, that carries into the flavour, where the complex fruit flavours imparted by the hops are very powerful..

Liberty Ale

Brewery	Anchor
Strength (ABV)	6.0%
Description	Amber colour. Overpowering citric aroma, which leads to a more rounded fruity hoppiness that stays to the end.

THE BEER DIRECTORY

Strong Ales
(BOTTLED-CONDITIONED)

Many bottled beers that contain sediment are given a designated shelf life of about a year, similar to a filtered product. A few, including some of the stronger Belgian ales and those from Trappist monasteries, are recommended to be kept for longer periods before being drunk. In the UK, the four such beers that survived the melt-down in breweries after the Second World War fall into this category. White Shield is covered above under 'Pale Ale' (see p. 146) and Imperial Russian Stout is dealt with under 'Imperial Stout' (see p. 200). That leaves Thomas Hardy Ale and Prize Old Ale, each distinguished enough to be highlighted individually.

Introduced by Gale's brewery of Hampshire just after the First World War, Prize Old Ale was based on a barley wine recipe brought from

Hardy's Ale

Brewery	Thomas Hardy
Strength (ABV)	12.0%
Description	Ruby colour. Full texture, sweetish port wine taste becomes more complex and vinous after five years, with a range of fruit flavours.

Yorkshire. After a conventional fermentation of a week, it matures for up to twelve months and then matures a further three months in the bottle, sealed with old-fashioned corks, before being sent out for sale. The nominal strength is 9.0% ABV: as with most beers that work in the bottle, this can increase with age – the drink-by date is five years from bottling, but many recommend up to 20 years, or even longer.

Thomas Hardy's Ale was first brewed in 1968 by Eldridge Pope (since renamed the Thomas Hardy Brewery) of Dorset, in honour of that county's renowned poet-novelist. It matures for six months and is bottled with its natural yeast. Hardy's Ale has no recommended drink-by date; the strength is given as 12.0% ABV, probably an estimated average based on the original gravity of 1125. The bottles used to be both nip-sized and numbered, but it now sells in 275 ml/0.5 pint bottles with just the year of bottling on the label.

Prize Old Ale

Brewery	Gale
Strength (ABV)	9.0%
Description	Ruby-brown colour. Fruity aroma. Complex, vinous-toffee flavour that becomes very pronounced in the finish.

Trappist Ales

These six breweries represent a closed order, in more than one sense. They are set in Trappist monasteries – five in Belgium, the other just over the border in Holland – in which the monks do the brewing. Although each is independent and produces distinct ales, they cooperate with each other. One manifestation of this is the use of the word 'Trappist' for their beers, a right bestowed upon no other brewery.

Monks have traditionally been brewers, as a means of fortifying themselves with vitamins as well as to avoid the hazards attached to drinking untreated water. They also use the revenue from sales for the benefit of the monastery, in some cases to finance essential building. The beers sold are powerful and heavy, but monks usually make weaker versions for their own consumption.

None of today's Trappist abbeys can show an unbroken history of brewing. Orval, founded in 1070 and the oldest of the six, was destroyed more than once, notably during the French Revolution, and started brewing again in the 1930s after being empty for more than a hundred years. A similar story can be told about Rochefort. The other monasteries started brewing in the 19th century.

By agreed definition, Trappist beers for sale are top-fermented ales that re-ferment in the bottle, which gives them a shelf life of at least three years. They also have to be brewed within the walls of a Trappist abbey. The so-called 'abbey' beers (see p.112) are monastery-style ales, possibly produced by commercial brewers under licence. Until recently, a close relationship of this kind involved an existing Trappist brew-monastery, the Abbey St Sixtus at Westvleteren near the French border with Belgium. The smallest of the six, its three beers do not travel widely, but it did allow similar products under the St Sixtus banner (but with-out the cachet of the Trappist name) to be brewed down the road by the St. Bernardus brewery.

Apart from Orval, with just the one beer of that name, the Trappist brewers generally produce at least three for sale. The largest of them, Westmalle, categorize their beers of, respectively, 6.0% and 9.0% ABV as Dubbel and Tripel (their weakest beer, Extra, is drunk mostly within the monastery), and these terms have passed into common use, though found more

Orval	
Brewery	Abbaye d'Orval
Strength (ABV)	6.2%
Description	Amber-gold colour. Sour-apple aroma. Softish texture, yeasty, slightly sour with a definite hoppy tang that remains prominent to the finish.

Chimay Rouge (Belgium) • 7.0% ABV

among the abbey beers than among the other Trappists. Chimay beers from De Scourmont are colour-coded Rouge, Blanche and Bleue, in ascending order of strength, while Rochefort simply employs the numbers 6, 8 and 10 to represent the degree of gravity – a Belgian system that works out slightly under the percentage of alcohol by volume (the mighty Rochefort 10, for instance, weighs in at 11.3% ABV). But in Holland, the La Trappe beers of Koningshoeven climb from Dubbel to Tripel to Quadrupel.

There are differences as well as similarities between beers of comparable strengths and nomenclature, just as every mild and bitter is not intended to taste the same. But each is the result of a complex brewing and maturation process, notably in the use of different yeasts and in the way sugar, in the form of

Trappistes Rochefort 8

Brewery	Abbaye Saint Rémy
Strength (ABV)	9.2%
Description	Dark copper colour. Full texture, roast-coffee bitterness, leading to bitter-sweet finish.

La Trappe (Netherlands)
• 6.5% ABV

liquid candy, may be added during the conditioning maturation cycle to encourage further fermentation. What most have in common is a full body and a heavy, but not over-sweet palate, the taste hanging around enticingly long after the beer goes down.

Elsewhere, monasteries brewing and selling commercially can be found in Germany and Austria.

WHEAT BEERS

Bavarian Pale Wheat Beers

One of the traditional Bavarian styles, top-fermenting wheat beers were considered very much a modern-day speciality, brewed in small quantities until a sudden upsurge gave them around 30% of the (very substantial) state market. Unlike Belgian wheat beers inspired by Hoegaarden, whose wheat is unmalted, these are brewed with malted wheat, mixed with the malted barley during the mash in at least equal proportions – usually the wheat takes precedence and, in Germany, a beer only earns the description *weizen* if wheat forms at least half the mash.

Even if actual spices are not added, as they are to Hoegaarden Witbier, the wheat does impart fruity or clove-like flavours to the final product. The hop varieties are chosen mainly for their preservative qualities. After fermentation, the beer is often filtered and a fresh yeast added to allow the beer to re-ferment in the bottle. Interestingly, some breweries prefer to use a lager-type bottom-fermenting yeast for the secondary fermentation; this clings to the bottom of the bottle and gives the drinker some control over how much yeast floats in the glass.

Two names most often cited are Schneider, whose Schneider Weisse is very highly regarded, and

Erdinger, whose wheat beers outsell all others in Germany. But such well-known firms as Spaten, Löwenbräu, Kaltenberg, Paulaner, Maisel and Hopf (which, despite its name, brews nothing but unhoppy, if excellent, wheat beers) are also substantial brewers in the style.

Incidentally, the German words *weisse* and *weizen* mean, respectively 'white' and 'wheat'. A wheat beer with sediment may be called a weisse, to describe its appearance, or a weizen to describe its contents.

To complicate matters even more, wheat beers are sometimes served without the wheat, which has been filtered out. Some of the soft and fruity flavours are

Schneider Weisse

Brewery	Schneider
Strength (ABV)	5.4%
Description	Amber colour. Smoked-herring aroma. Full texture, malty, slightly dry with a pronounced smoky aftertaste.

lost as a result, but what you get is a clean-tasting beer with a captivatingly dry tang quite unlike that of a weisse beer. The market leader is probably Erdinger's Kristall – with German wheat beers, *Hefe* (yeast) often appears on the label to indicate the beer has not been filtered, while the word *Kristall* implies a clear beer. In Britain, the Hop Back brewery produces an enticing version known as Thunderstorm (5.0% ABV). Wheat beers of all styles are now increasingly brewed in the UK and the USA.

Franziskaner

Brewery	Spaten
Strength (ABV)	5.0%
Description	Pale cloudy colour.
	Fruity, slightly smoked aroma.
	Soft texture, slightly sweet apple-cloves
	flavour and a sweetish aftertaste.

Belgian Wheat Beers

Apart perhaps from Germany, Belgium can boast the best record in brewing continuity. One that almost got away for a time was the tradition of brewing pale, cloudy, spiced wheat beers, *witbier*. These had virtually disappeared from the wheat-growing area directly to the east of Brussels, which is where you find the village of Hoegaarden. There, the style was revived in 1965 by Pierre Celis, who named his brewery De Kluis 'cloister' in honour of the village's monastic/brewing past. After being nearly destroyed by fire in 1985, De Kluis has been scrupulously expanded and modernized and is now run by Interbrew, who claim to be the world's fourth-largest brewing group. Celis has since moved to the USA, where he brews his own excellent wheat beers near Austin in Texas

Hoegaarden and similar Belgian products differ from the German weisse beers most notably in the use of unmalted wheat. They are often spiced, in Hoegaarden's case with coriander, dried orange peel and curaçao, all of which help to produce strong flavours. After the copper boil, where the hops provide protection and some aroma rather than bitterness, the beer is fermented for five days, conditioned for two to three weeks and then re-fermented, in bottle or keg, with a fresh yeast.

The international success of Hoegaarden White Beer has encouraged breweries in other parts of Belgium to join in. Riva's Dentergem, De Gouden Boom's Brugs Tarwebier and Van Honsebrouck's Blanchke are among the witbiers from Flanders, while they are also

Hoegaarden White Beer

Brewery	Interbrew
Strength (ABV)	5.0%
Description	Pale and cloudy. Light fruit aroma. Strong herbal taste, with cloves coming through and a touch of orange.

brewed in the French-speaking south by Silly (Titje) and Du Bocq (Blanche de Namur). Strength is usually around 5.0% ABV. Apart from a few in the Netherlands (and Texas), wheat-beer brewers outside Belgium usually follow the German models.

Dentergems Wit Bier

Brewery	Riva
Strength (ABV)	5.0%
Description	Pale and cloudy. Fruity aroma, with cloves. Quite a tart, hoppy taste, with hint of banana.

Berliner Weisse

The wheat beers associated with Berlin are among the more idiosyncratic, closer in conception to a Belgian beer than most of Germany's products. Perhaps that is why the style, once quite common in northern Germany, is now confined to the capital, with a few survivors elsewhere. Its survival in Berlin itself was not helped by the city's post-war division, but it still retains an appeal for many locals.

The mash contains up to about 50% malted wheat, generally below that of Bavarian wheat beers. The hops used hardly impart any bitterness and the final strength, about 3.0% ABV, is very low by German standards. What sets Berliner Weisse apart is the addition of a lactic culture, developed many years ago in Berlin itself, that interacts with the yeast during the fermen-

Schultheiss Berliner Weisse

Brewery	Schultheiss
Strength (ABV)	3.7%
Description	Pale, cloudy colour. Strong pear-like aroma. Soft texture, very sharp sour-acid taste that grows more rounded after a year's careful storage.

tation. In another hint of Belgian practice, one of the two main producers, Schultheiss, blends the fresh wort with an older version.

After a few months' maturation, a second dose of top-fermenting yeast is added and the beer conditions in the bottle for a further month. The resulting beer is soft in texture but with a sharp, citric sourness that Berliners often tone down with a dash of syrup.

Hints of the style are found elsewhere, notably the Bremer Weisse (3.0% ABV), produced in that city by Haake-Beck and the Pinkus HefeWeizen (a bit strong at 5.0% ABV) from Munster's Pinkus Müller brewery. Their Alt, at 5.1% ABV, is much stronger than a

Berliner Weisse, but it is brewed from a 40%-wheat mash, and a touch of lactic culture during conditioning helps to produce a most distinctive beer.

Pinkus Hefe Weizen

Brewer	Pinkus Müller
Strength (ABV)	5.0%
Description	Cloudy pale colour. Light pear aroma. Very smooth texture, nutty-pear flavour that dominates throughout.

Faro

Surely, adding sugar to a glass of beer and stirring it up, the way you sweeten tea or coffee, is the ultimate sacrilege? In the case of sour lambic-based beers from Belgium, the practice at least makes some sense. Not that long ago, lambics were the favoured tipple around Brussels and it was quite common for the taste to be softened, perhaps with nothing more than water, for those who preferred not to drink the unadulterated form. The practice is still found in cafes and restaurants.

Timmermans Faro
(Belgium)• 3.5% ABV

However, as well as producing fruit lambics, a few brewers and blenders also produce what is called a *faro*. A young lambic, sometimes taken from the weaker wort after mashing in cases where there is more than one run, always forms the base. Sugar, traditionally in candied form, is added at the brewery, and the beer is pasteurized when bottled so as to ,preserve the desired level of sweetness by stopping the sugar from causing any further fermentation. Faros by Boon, Cantillon, Vander Linden, Timmermans and Lindemans are among those on sale today. The strength is normally around 5.0%, no different from other lambic beers, though at one time, a low-gravity faro called *mars* was brewed.

Lindemans Lambic Faro

Brewery	Lindemans
Strength (ABV)	4.7%
Description	Copper-coloured. Soft texture, sweet taste over a tangy background

---

Framboise

Apart from krieks, the most commonly satisfying of the lambic-based fruit beers are made with raspberries, known as *framboise* (French) and *frambozen* (Flemish), because they have a flavour both sharp and sweet that can blend with the lambic – the process is, or should be, very similar, with whole fruit being added to the fermentation. The best examples of framboise and kriek change character with age, being sweeter through the natural fruit flavour at the start and more tangy after about a year, with the framboises imparting a taste that is perhaps more rounded without becoming sickly.

Timmermans Framboise (Belgium) • 4.0% ABV.

Many lambic brewers now produce range of fruit flavours. Whatever the sales, these are often less successful from an idealistic viewpoint, especially when both the sweetness dominates and the alcohol level drops to 3.0% ABV or below (the best lambic-based fruit beers are usually around 5.0%). Blackcurrant, peaches and bananas are among the ingredients used. Non-lambic fruit beers are dealt with below.

Framboise Girardin

Brewery	Girardin
Strength (ABV)	5.0%
Description	Smooth, red-coloured, raspberry-flavoured, with a slight acid bitterness that lingers.

Fruit Beers

Liefmans Kriek (Belgium)
• 6.5% ABV

Florisgaarden Ninkeberry (Belgium)
• 4.5% ABV

Descriptions such as *kriek* and *frambozen* signify a lambic-based fruit beer. There are other beers made with fruit that have little or no connection with lambic. In Belgium, the Huyghe brewery makes wheat beers with very strong and clean flavours, including cherry and strawberry. Although only 3.0% ABV, they are clearly marketed as beers and should not be confused with so-called 'alcopops'. Some smaller American brewers, such as Marin near San Francisco, make strongish beers with similar characteristics, the rich fruit flavours dominating.

As noted earlier, Liefmans produce kriek and frambozen beers in which the the basic brown ale is blended and re-fermented with fruit. The results are closer to the lambic style than to other fruit beers. Exactly the same applies to Rodenbach's Alexander, for which cherry essence is added to the Grand Cru.

The Heather Ale company of Scotland has produced Grozet, a wheat beer of 5.0% ABV that is spiced with bog myrtle and then fermented with gooseberries (see also 'Rye/Spiced Beers', p.206).

Liefmans Frambozenbier

Brewery	Liefmans
Strength (ABV)	4.5%
Description	Red-brown colour. Smooth texture underpins the very rounded taste of raspberry.

Gueuze

When British beer drinkers order a mild-and-bitter, a light-and-bitter or any combination of two beers, they are blending. Some brewers systematically mix different brews. This can be done in various ways: after fermentation, for instance, or by dividing wort from the mash tun into 'strong' and 'weak' runs (the weaker run is the result of a second sparging of the grist with hot water, as a tea pot can be refilled with hot water to produce a further, weaker brew) boiling them separately and then blending to produce two or more beers of notably different strengths.

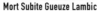

Mort Subite Gueuze Lambic

Brewery	Alken-Maes
Strength (ABV)	4.3%
Description	Amber colour. Light pear-apple aroma. Smooth, slightly oily texture, sweet-sour taste with apple undertones; more character (i.e. sourness) in the unfiltered version.

The most complex example of mixing two beers to produce a third comes from Belgium in the production of *gueuze*. In simple terms, to make a gueuze you blend an old with a young lambic. In practice, several casks of each may need to be mixed together before the blender is satisfied. Having decided that a cask should form the basis of a blend rather than being sold as pure lambic, the blender than has to decide which lambics to blend it with. The best of them use a substantial proportion of lambics that are three years old: these provide most of the flavour, whereas the younger lambics are needed mainly because they still contain enough carbon

Cantillon Gueuze Lambic

Brewery	Cantillon
Strength (ABV)	5.0%
Description	Yellow-amber colour. Quite smooth texture, sour tang with a complex range of fruit flavours, also present in the aftertaste.

dioxide to impart sparkle and to enable the resultant blend to re-ferment. A top-quality gueuze will be conditioned at source for at least a few months before being released for sale.

Some brands are sweetened to such an extent that the tart flavours are over-compromised. These products sell well, but a true gueuze should have a sour (though never acetic) taste.

Kriek

The Flemish word for cherries gives its name to arguably the most satisfying of all lambic-based fruit beers. A proper *kriek* should taste tart and sour: the sweetness imparted by the cherry adds roundness almost as an afterthought, though the perfect match between lambic and cherry, sour and sweet, is what makes kriek so irresistible.

Some deliberately aim for a sweeter taste on the commercial grounds that the public demands it. In those cases, much of the cherry content will be provided by fruit juice or extract. A true kriek should

Timmermans Kriek Lambic

Brewery	Timmermans
Strength (ABV)	5.0%
Description	Bronze-red colour. Cherry flavour erupts from the slightly tart, sour palette that lingers on.

contain whole cherries, added to the fermenting lambic so as to play a full part in the maturation process. The fruit sugars themselves join in the active fermentation, as do the younger lambics mixed in by the brewer/blender, while both skins and stones contribute to the final flavour.

There are krieks that cover the entire spectrum. Those under the Belle Vue name tend to play down the sharpness. Cantillon is among the most uncompromising, Timmermans and Mort Subite come somewhere in the middle, while Boon's kriek has the fullest fruit flavours.

Lambic

The town of Lembeek, once a place of strategic importance and briefly independent, has given its name to a *lambic* style – unique today but resembling the primordial state of the art of brewing. This can be found around the area of Payottenland, west of Brussels in the valley of the Senne River, where most lambics are brewed. Instead of keeping yeast under strict scientific control, brewers let the beer, still cooling after a very long boil, pick up the wild yeasts floating through the air.

GRAND CRU

CANTILLON

| OLD LAMBIC | | INGREDIENTS WHEAT MALT HOPS |

BRUOCSELLA 1900

BR. CANTILLON 1900 BRUXELLES – BIERE BIO – BR. GEUZE BIER   ALC 5 % VOL ℮ 37,5 cl.

Cantillon Lambic

Brewery	Cantillon
Strength (ABV)	5.0%
Description	Light brown colour. Sharp but warming vinous taste, like very good barley wine, with a strong sour finish.

Even earlier in the process, there are other divergences from today's brewing methods. At Cantillon, one of the most traditional brewers, the grist for mashing contains about 35% unmalted wheat to 65% malted barley, and the copper boil that follows lasts over three hours rather than 90 minutes. The other major difference in the boil involves the hops. These tend to be withered, flavourless and at least three years old, because the hop in lambic brewing retains its original function of acting as a preservative, whereas the flavour qualities of fresh hops would not go well with the sour, often vinous taste of true lambic.

The beer cools in a wide but shallow pan, while wild yeast from outside slips through the slats in the roof. It is then transferred to oak casks that once contained wine or port, and conditions in these casks for up to three years. Unlike the super-hygienic atmosphere found in other breweries, scruffiness is the rule, to encourage the wild yeasts. Cantillon welcomes spiders, for their webs and because they kill insects trying to get at the casks.

Weizenbock/Dunkelweizen

The stronger versions of wheat beers are given the traditional 'bock' terminology and may be labelled as '*Weizenbocks*'. They will generally be above 7.0% ABV, usually dark in colour and be most in demand during the colder winter months.

As with dark wheat beers of lesser strength, these are common in Bavaria without being overwhelmingly represented in the export market. Among the bigger

Schneider Aventinus

Brewery	Schneider
Strength (ABV)	8.0%
Description	Red-brown colour. Spiced coffee aroma. Full texture, fruit-chocolate with smoky undertone. Bitter-sweet aftertaste.

names, the Erdinger brewery's smooth-tasting Pikantus contrasts with Schneider's Aventinus (slightly stronger at 7.7% ABV, and billed as a Weizen Doppelbock), of a similar red-brown colour but heavier and with a more spicy taste.

As with non-wheat lagers, the Bavarians also brew dark versions of their wheat beers. Often called *Dunkelweizen* or *dunkel Weissbier*, these may contain a porportion of malted wheat that has been darkened by roasting and will differ from the paler version as dark lagers differ from light (or old ales from

ErdingerDunkel Weissbier

Brewery	Erdinger
Strength (ABV)	5.6%
Description	Brown-red colour.
	Light apple-clove aroma. Malty flavour
	with hint of chocolate. Smooth yet full texture.

premium bitters). Some of the edge imparted by the wheat is offset by full, round flavours from the darkened malts, the result being less fruity .

Erdinger's Dunkel Weissbier is among the few widely available outside Germany, and one may also find Spaten's Franziskaner Dunkel. But within Bavaria itself, breweries of all sizes produce excellent examples, one being the Weissbier from Prince Luitpold of the Kaltenberg Brewery.

PORTER & STOUTS

Porter

Porters and stouts belong to the family of top-fermented, dark beers that preceded the IPAs and light-coloured bitters as the favoured tipple of pub-goers. Differences between the two styles may not be readily apparent to the casual drinker. Both have bitter, roasted flavours, and neither come in a specific strength: in general, porters are slightly sweeter and stouts more full-bodied.

King & Barnes
Old Porter (UK)
• 5.5% ABV

The rise of porter is usually traced to London during the 18th century, when the brewing industry was beginning to change from small units such as pubs to what became the regional and, later, national brewers with large tied estates. A popular beer was a blend of pale ale with both fresh and stale dark ale, the staleness giving a slightly tart, lactic taste much admired at the time. Porter became synonymous with 'entire', the term used for a beer that was not a three-way blend but was brewed as an 'Entire Butt' to give a similar effect.

Recreating a porter based on one of their own recipes from the 1850s, Harvey's Brewery in Sussex used the identical roasted malts, boiled for three hours to ensure stability, and stored the beer in sealed vats that kept the

Samuel Smith Taddy Porter (UK)
•5.0% ABV

beer alive by retaining the carbon dioxide given off. This is how porters would have been preserved in the breweries for about a year, with beer drawn off from the vats as required. Dry and acrid to begin with, the beer mellows in taste and texture during the storage period in the way that a well-hopped IPA would have matured by the time the troops drank it. Also, the sweeter edge to the aftertaste exists because another characteristic is the amount of residual sugar left after fermentation, so that the beer brewed at a gravity of 1054 drops to about 4.5% ABV.

Since the revival in differing styles of beer, porter has once more become generally available in the UK, on both a regular and a seasonal basis. The same applies to the USA. Until then, almost the only porter brewed regularly came from such Scandinavian firms as Pripps in Sweden, Synebrychoff in Finland (with

Original Porter

Brewery	Shepherd Neame
Strength (ABV)	5.2%
Description	Dark ruby colour. Slightly vinous aroma. Smooth texture, roasted chocolate flavour, with underlying hoppiness, and a sharp coffee aftertaste.

Koff's Porter) and Tuborg in Denmark, even if none was exactly mass-marketed.

Koff Porter

Brewer	Sinebrychoff
Strength (ABV)	7.2%
Description	Very dark brown-black colour. Faint pear-chocolate aroma. Soft texture, powerful chocolate-roast flavour leading to a coffee-chocolate finish.

Dry Stout

Murphy's Irish Stout
(Ireland) • 4.0% ABV

Whereas the origin of the name 'porter' probably arose because of the beer's popularity with porters who worked in London's markets (there are conflicting theories), 'stout' began as a term of alcoholic strength, used to distinguish the stronger beers emerging from a particular brewery. The drink that became what the world knows as Guinness began as Extra Stout Porter. Then, the exported version became Foreign Extra Stout, and it is this beer that eventually took over.

Guinness were always export-minded and, like the IPA brewers, they used plenty of hops to help preserve their beers as they travelled long distances by canal and by sea. This probably accounts for the extra bitterness linked to stout. Some of the roasted barley Guinness brewed with was unmalted, which gave their stout its dry sharpness that, again, one does not normally associate with porter.

Guinness, in several variations of the basic Irish brew highlighted below, continues to be available throughout the world. Ireland remains the centre for stout, with the local rivals of Guinness, Murphy's and

Beamish & Crawford, picking up fast after decades of being wholly dominated by the world giant. Murphy's stout is the softest, least bitter of the three, while Beamish's has a rounded, milk-coffee flavour.

The new generation of brewing companies in the UK and the USA often include a stout in their portfolios. Throughout the rest of the brewing world, it has never gone away even if, against strict tradition, the method of brewing may involve bottom fermentation. Carlsberg produce an Imperial Stout Porter; in Japan, Asahi and Kirin brew stouts of 8.0% ABV. The most remarkable survivor comes from the Ceylon Brewery in Sri Lanka, whose Lion Stout (6.2% ABV and available in bottle-conditioned form) is both top-fermented and, in a couple of bars, served traditionally from handpumps. Another bottle-conditioned gem comes from the long-established Cooper's brewery of Adelaide, Australia (Cooper's Extra Stout, 6.8% ABV).

Guinness Extra Stout

Brewery	Guinness
Strength (ABV)	4.3%
Description	Dark-brown colour. Creamy texture, assertively dry, roasted coffee flavour, leading to a balanced, bitter finish.

Imperial Stout

Another instance of beer brewed to survive long distances, this concerns a stout that travelled in hogsheads to Russia and the Baltic Sea area from Britain. The trade begain in the 1780s and lasted until the Bolsheviks took over. By then, a similar beer was

Samuel Smith Imperial
Stout (UK)• 7.0% ABV

being brewed in Russia, allegedly cashing in on that British stout's popularity, though the new regime soon put a stop to this.

The original brewery – Barclay's of London, later taken over by Courage – is hardly more important to the legend than the man who bottled and exported Imperial Extra Double Stout, a Belgian named A. Le Coq. He donated 5000 bottles to local hospitals and was given a Royal Warrant by the grateful Russians. Thus honoured, Imperial Russian Stout was continued by Courage as a highly specialized beer, one of a handful (see 'Strong Ales', p.160) that is brewed to be stored for several years.

At 10.0% ABV, fermented down from an original gravity of 1098, it could be described as a barley wine. Currently brewed most recently by Scottish-Courage at John Smith's in Yorkshire (they stopped brewing it in 1998), it develops a ripe, sherry-like flavour that improves with age – the recommended drink-by date is five years from the brewing date on the bottle, but many keep it longer.

A rival Imperial Stout, at 7.0% ABV and first brewed in the 1980s , comes from the Samuel Smith brewery at Tadcaster, coincidentally (or not) a few hundred yards from John Smith's. This is also a rich, complex brew, though without the laying-down properties that make Imperial Russian unique. The tradition of powerful stouts and porters remains strong in the Baltic countries.

Imperial Russian Stout

Brewery	Scottish-Courage
Strength (ABV)	10.0%
Description	Black-brown colour. Full texture, warming, well-balanced, chocolate-malt taste that becomes sharper with age.

Sweet Stout

A brewery long since gone, Mackeson & Co. from Kent, still gives its name to what is now almost a unique beer. The idea of adding lactose sugar – produced by dairies as part of the process by which they make cheese – to the wort as it boils in the copper was inspired, the brewery claimed, because of its nutritional value. Such beers were once known widely as 'milk stouts' and, especially before the introduction of lactose, were probably drunk with the milk added according to taste.

Mackeson

Brewery	Whitbread
Strength (ABV)	3.0%
Description	Dark brown colour.
	Slight chocolate aroma.
	Soft texture, lactic dried-milk taste.

In today's more strict labelling climate, 'milk stout' as a term is frowned upon, as are claims to good health. Mackeson eventually ended up being owned by Whitbread, who have continued to produce the bottled stout at their modern plant in Lancashire. By repute, those who still seek it are elderly ladies popping into the pub for a pre-lunch tipple. It is a suitably warming drink, chocolate-coffee flavoured and hardly bitter. Because the lactose does not ferment, Mackeson stout ends up rather weaker than its original gravity of 1050 would suggest. It sells enough to make it worthwhile, and there is a considerable export trade, for which the finished beer is a lot stronger (5.0% ABV, as against 3.0%).

Another survival can be found on the Mediterranean island of Malta where Farson's make their very dark Lacto Milk Stout. Also a mere 3.0% ABV in strength, and containing vitamin B, it is still regarded as a health product.

Oatmeal & Oyster Stouts

Some regard stout made, in part, from oatmeal as another attempt to boost the health-giving properties of beer. As happened all too often during the concentration of brewing after 1950, the brand eventually disappeared, to re-emerge later when interest in different styles of beer made breweries think hard about broadening their portfolios.

Scottish Oatmeal Stout (UK)
• 4.2% ABV

The first example of modern times was the Oatmeal Stout from the Samuel Smith brewery in North Yorkshire. It has the characteristic smoothness, blending the expected coffee flavours with a touch of porridge and, at 5.0% ABV, is about as strong as you get in this style. Not surprisingly, the revival has been particularly keen in Scotland, with Maclay of Alloa (Oat Malt Stout) and Broughton of Biggar (Scottish Oatmeal Stout) joining in. As the name implies, Maclay's stout is made with malted oats that impart an especially rounded, less bitter taste.

Another revived tradition has been the return of oyster stouts. In their original form, these may or may

Marston's Oyster Stout (UK)
• 4.5% ABV

not have included oysters in the recipe: some brewers undoubtedly did use them, but the term also reflected the culinary (and health-giving) relationship of the two ingredients, oysters and stout both being a common part of the average diet in London and Dublin. Of the revivalists, Marston's Oyster Stout does not actually contain any oyster-derived product, although Murphy's Oyster Stout, brewed by Whitbread in England, does add oyster-juice to the boil.

Samuel Smith Oatmeal Stout

Brewery	Samuel Smith
Strength (ABV)	5.0%
Description	Dark- brown colour.
	Soft texture with chocolate-coffee flavours
	that dominate and carry on in the aftertaste.

SPECIALITY BEERS
Rye and Spiced beers

A traditional German style revived some years ago by Schierlinger in Bavaria is beer which includes rye in the mash. Schierlinger Roggen (*Roggen* is the German for 'rye') has many of the characters of a wheat beer, and an even smoother texture.

Rye has long been a part of beverages, including beer, in Scandinavia and the Baltic countries, and is usually included in the making of the Finnish *sahti*. A traditional drink, and still something of a cottage industry, sahti is flavoured with juniper berries and filtered through juniper twigs that impart a soft cinnamon/cloves flavour to the beer. The most readily available version, from the Lammin brewery, comes in wine-type boxes and is around 8.0% ABV.

Spices in beer pre-dated the widespread use of hops. Reviving an old Scottish tradition, the Heather Ale company has produced Fraoch to a recipe from the 16th century, in which heather flowers take the place of hops.

Some Belgian ales that fall in the strong and pale category add a spice or two. Hoegaarden's Forbidden Fruit and Huyghe's Delerium Tremens, which conditions in an opaque and highly decorated bottle, both derive distinctive flavours from the addition of coriander.

C'est aux temps reculés où la bière s'appelait encore cervoise que la Barbār a puisé ses racines. La Barbār est née d'un mélange subtil des substances les plus fortes et d'arômes les plus délicats...

De wortels van Barbār zijn te vinden in vervlogen tijden toen het bier nog 'Cervoise' heette. Barbār is ontstaan uit een subtiele mengeling van de meest uitgesproken substanties en verfijnde aroma's...

Barbār

Bière Spéciale blonde au Miel
Speciaal Blond Honing Bier

arbar (Belgium)
• 8.0% ABV

Honey-flavoured ales have become increasingly available on draught from the newer British breweries. From Belgium, the Lefèbvre brewery produces the strong (8.0% ABV) Barbar in bottled form.

Schierlinger Roggen

Brewery	Schierlinger
Strength (ABV)	4.9%
Description	Red-brown colour. Very soft, creamy texture. Hint of cloves, sweet with a lingering tang of fruit.

Delerium Tremens

Brewer	Huyghe Melle
Strength (ABV)	9.0%
Description	Golden colour.
	Banana-nutty aroma.
	Soft, slightly oily texture, strong flavour
	of bitter almonds, with hints of fruit, that
	builds to a slightly dry finish.

Seasonal Beers

Brewing beers to be drunk at a certain time has been a feature of the industry for centuries. Before modern techniques of refrigeration, summer brewing was hazardous at best, which led to the Saisons of Belgium, the Bières de Garde of France and the Märzens of Bavaria. However, the general principle of festive beers or of beers brewed for a special occasion has always been present and, in recent years, has made a powerful commercial impact on the scene in the UK and elsewhere.

Christmas brings many specials, including one of the strongest. Samichlaus, a dark brown lager dedicated to St. Nicholas (Santa Claus), is brewed by the Swiss company Hürlimann on the appropriate Saint's Day (6 December) and is only released at the

King & Barnes Christmas Ale
(UK) • 8.0% ABV

same time the following year. Regrettably, it was last brewed in 1996 and may not appear again. In the UK, Christmas specials often appear in draught form alongside the old ales, usually stronger and available only around the turn of the year. In Belgium, the Netherlands and the Scandinavian countries, bottled products are common.

The innovative Anchor brewery of San Francisco set a trend by introducing a special beer for Thanksgiving Day (the last Thursday in November) that remains available until the end of the year. The recipe is different each time.

Samichlaus

Brewery	Hürlimann
Strength (ABV)	14.0%
Description	Dark ruby colour. Heavy vinous aroma. Sharp, roasted malt flavour, port with a touch of armagnac.

Draught beers produced for a particular season, by the month (Bateman's have named a series after the signs of the zodiac), for a beer festival and, to satisfy a growing demand for new beers, simply on an ad hoc basis are very much a part of the current UK scene. Among a clutch of harvest ales, brewed in September from new crops of malted barley and/or hops, the strong bottled Harvest Ale from Lees (11.5% ABV) stands out. Others include Wadworth's Malt & Hops and King & Barnes Harvest Ale.

King & Barnes Harvest Ale

Brewer	King & Barnes
Strength (ABV)	4.7%
Description	Amber-russet colour. Strong apple aroma. Soft texture, malty base, with sharp citric overtones, dry but fruity aftertaste.

Millennium Ale (UK) • 9.5% ABV

Appendices

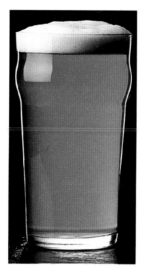

GLOSSARY

Words that appear in SMALL CAPITALS indicate other terms that appear in the glossary in which additional details or explanations are given.

Alcohol by volume (ABV)

An indicator of beer strength, measured by the percentage of alcohol in the finished product. It is often abbreviated to ABV.

Ale

Refers today to any type of beer brewed by the TOP FERMENTATION method.

Alpha acid

The ingredient of the hop plant that gives bitterness to beer.

Boiling

The process by which the WORT is boiled after MASHING to allow added ingredients (notably hops) to impart their flavours.

Bottle-conditioned

A term used to describe a beer that continues to mature in the bottle, thanks to active yeasts or sugars that remain in the liquid during the bottling process.

These continue to ferment while the beer is on the shelf, so allowing it's flavour and strength to develop. See BREWERY-CONDITIONED, CASK-CONDITIONED.

Bottom fermentation

One of the two PRIMARY FERMENTATION methods, during which the yeast sinks to the bottom of the fermenting vessel. This is the technqiue used in the production of lagers. See TOP FERMENTATION.

Brewery-conditioned

A term used to describe a beer which is filtered, and usually pasteurized, before being packaged in the brewery. See BOTTLE-CONDITIONED, CASK-CONDITIONED.

Brewpub

A pub with its own brewery producing beer for consumption on the premises.

Carbon dioxide (CO_2)

The gas given off during fermentation, without which the beer would become flat. If a beer is rendered lifeless by pasteurisation, CO_2 has to be added.

Cask

A barrel containing beer that undergoes SECONDARY FERMENTATION after leaving the brewery. The term is often used as a shorthand to mean CASK-CONDITIONED beers.

Cask-conditioned

Beer that has not been filtered after the primary fermentation but continues to ferment in the barrel (cask) after being racked and therefore to produce its own CARBON DIOXIDE.

Conditioning

The process following PRIMARY FERMENTATION when the beer matures in the brewery, usually by being stored under controlled temperatures. This is an essential part of the BOTTOM FERMENTATION process. See BOTTLE-CONDITIONED, BREWERY-CONDITIONED, CASK-CONDITIONED.

Copper

A term sometimes used synonymously with BOILING, because the boiling vessels were traditionally made of copper.

Decoction mashing

A system of MASHING in which parts of the mash are separated from the main batch, heated in a separate vessel and at higher temperatures before being brought together again at the end of the process. This system maximises the conversion of starch to sugar, while dispersing elements that might harm the beer. See INFUSION MASH

217

G L O S S A R Y

Dry-hopping

The technique of adding hops to the beer after the BOILING is completed, often at cask-racking stage, as a means of imparting extra flavours.

Fermentation

The addition of living yeast to the brew that produces alcohol.

Hop

The plant that, added to the boil, imparts bitterness and other flavours, as well as preservative qualities.

Infusion mashing

A system of MASHING whereby crushed malt is mixed with hot water and left to stew, during which time the starch in the malt converts to sugar. See DECOCTION MASH

Keg

A barrel designed to stay upright in the cellar (as opposed to the horizontal, belly-flopping cask). The term is also used as shorthand for BREWERY-CONDITIONED beer.

Kettle

The same as COPPER.

Krausen

The German practice of adding a small amount of unfermented WORT to beer that has already fermented, thus producing a further fermentation and extra CARBON DIOXIDE.

Lager

A widely adopted term used to describe pale-coloured beers produced by BOTTOM FERMENTATION, but which should apply to similar beers of any colour.

Liquor

The technical term for the water used in brewing.

Mashing

The process of extracting sugars from the malt by prolonged immersion in heated water. See DECOCTION MASH, INFUSION MASH.

Maturation

Another term for CONDITIONING.

Mixed-Gas

A system by which beer is preserved in and/or dispensed from a keg by a mixture of NITROGEN and CARBON DIOXIDE. See NITRO-KEG.

Nitrogen

Because it does not interact with the beer, nitrogen is increasingly being mixed with CARBON DIOXIDE as the gas used for blanket PRESSURE - as beer is drawn off, nitrogen fills the vacuum without carbonating what remains in the cask/keg.

Nitro-keg

A BREWERY-CONDITIONED ale, dispensed by the MIXED-GAS method. Nitrogen contributes to a creamy head on delivery while helping to preserve the beer without making it more gassy.

Original gravity (OG)

A measurement of the strength of a beer, calculated on the amount of fermentable matter, such as sugars, left in the WORT before yeast is added. Using this system, water is assigned a gravity of 1000, and any OG figure greater than this indicates the quantity of fermentable material used. The greater the amount of fermentable material, the more alcoholic (and thus stronger) will be the final product (e.g. an OG of 1080 is likely to produce a higher volume of alcohol after fermentation than 1040 OG).

Pressure

Casks may be subjected to top or blanket pressure. In a pub, beer pushed from the cellar to the bar counter by gas is being kept under top pressure. In a cask, if the gas – CARBON DIOXIDE or NITROGEN, or a mixture of the two - merely fills the vacuum caused by the egress of beer, the contents are being kept under blanket pressure.

Primary fermentation

The initial process whereby the WORT is converted into alcohol.

Racking

The stage in the brewing process when beer is transferred to casks or kegs for delivery outside the brewery. CASK-CONDITIONED beer transferred from one container to another after settling is described as racked beer. In the pub cellar, casks placed on-STILLAGE may be described as racked.

Secondary fermentation

Post-PRIMARY FERMENTATION, caused either by the original yeast not being filtered out or by yeast being freshly added. See BOTTLE-CONDITIONED, CASK-CONDITIONED.

Stillage

The racks in a pub cellar, where the beer is left to settle until ready to be dispensed.

Tanks

Some pub or club cellars contain metal tanks as

fixtures, capable of holding more than the largest cask, for beer transported in bulk. They are also used by BREW-PUBS, especially in the United States. The beer is usually filtered and/or protected by gas.

Top fermentation

One of the two PRIMARY FERMENTATION methods, during which the yeast rises to the top of the fermenting vessel. This is the technqiue used in the production of ales. See BOTTOM FERMENTATION.

Widget

A device fixed to the inside of a can of beer which releases nitrogen to help produce a smooth, creamy texture for the poured beer in the glass.

Wort

The unfermented liquid brew, in which sugars have been extracted via the mash.

Yeast

The living organism that interacts with the wort during fermentation and thereby turns it into an alcoholic product.

Zymurgy

Chemical term for beer fermentation, given widespread currency in the United States.

USEFUL ADDRESSES

A. Associations of Brewers

Trade associations in the major brewing countries, part of whose remit is to link with the public.

1. UNITED KINGDOM

Brewers and Licensed Retailers Association (BLRA)
42 Portman Square
London W1H 0BB
Tel: 0171-486 4831

Independent Family Brewers of Britain (IFBP)
3PR, Merchants Court
St Georges Street
Norwich NR3 1AB
Tel. 01603-619164

Society of Independent Brewers SIBA)
Ballards Brewery
The Old Sawmill
Nyewood
Petersfield
Hampshire GU31 5HA
Tel. 01730-821301

2. BELGIUM

Confereratie de Brouwerijen van Belgie (CBB)
Grote Market 10
1000 Brussel
Tel. 00 322 5114987

3. GERMANY

Deutscher Brauer-Bund e.v.
Po Box 20 04 52
Annabarger Str. 28
D-5300 Bonn
Tel: 00 49 228 959060

4. UNITED STATES OF AMERICA

Beer Institute
122C Street
NW. Suite 750
Washington DC 20001
Tel: 00 1 202 737 2337

American Homebrewers Association
736 Pearl St
Boulder
CO 80302
Tel. 00 1 303 477 0816

5. JAPAN

Brewers Association of Japan
ShowS Building 2-1-18 Kyobashi
Chuo-ku
Tokyo
Tel: 00 813 3561 8386

B. Consumer Organisations

1. UNITED KINGDOM

The Campaign for Real Ale Ltd (CAMRA)
230 Hatfield Road
St Albans
Hertfordshire AL1 4LW
England
Tel. 01727-867201

2. BELGIUM

Objectieve Bierproevers (OBP)
Postbus 32
2600 Bercham
Tel. 00 32 3 232 45 38

3. NETHERLANDS

Promotie Informatie Traditioneel Bier (PINT)
Postbus 3757
1001AN Amsterdam
Tel. (31) 252 522909

4. FRANCE

Les Amis De La Bière
5, Route de Mametz
62120 Aire-Sur-la Lys
Tel. 03 21 391452

5. NORWAY

Norsk Ølvenners Landsforbund (NØROL)
Postboks 6567 Etterstad
0607 Oslo
Tel. 0802 2324226

NB The European Beer Consumers Union (EBCU), which can be reached via CAMRA, includes the above, plus consumer organisations in Sweden, Finland, Estonia and Switzerland.

C. Mail Order

Many mail-order companies, especially in the US, operate as clubs, making their own decisions as to which beers are packaged. Those listed below should give the customer at least some discretion.

1. UNITED KINGDOM

The Beer Cellar
31 Norwich Road
Strumpshaw
Norwich
Norfolk NR13 4AG
Tel. 01603-714884

Beer Paradise
Unit 11
11 Riverside Place
Bridgewater Road
Leeds LS9 0RQ
Tel. 01132-359082

The Beer Shop
8 Pitfield Street
London N1 6HA
Tel. 0171-739 3701

2. MAINLAND EUROPE

Beer Around The World
30 Rue Bragance
L-1255 Luxembourg
Tel. 00 352 251849

3. USA

Ale In The Mail
121-22 Dupont Street
Plainview, NY 11803
Sales: 1-800-SEND-ALE (1-800-736-3253)
Customer Service: 1-800-708-0024

4. JAPAN

MicroBeers International
c/o Village Cellars Co. Ltd
1231 Shinbo
Himi, Toyama 935-02
Tel. 00 81 766 762881

APPENDICES

D. Beer on the Internet

APPENDICES

Three all-purpose sites, from which much specific detail on all aspects of beer and brewing worldwide can eventually be extracted:

http://www.breworld.com (Europe)

htpp://www.realbeer.com (USA)

http://www.beerinfo.com (USA)

For searches on beer-related subjects, a useful starting point is the Zymurgy Database:

http://www.arq.net/db/zymurgy

BEER FESTIVALS

Festivals offering a wide range of beers for sale – often with food, music and suitable side-shows also on hand – have become widespread. Below are listed a few national ones: full details of these, plus those of many regional and local festivals, should be available from the appropriate consumer association.

COUNTRY	CITY/TOWN	FESTIVAL	DATE
Belgium	Antwerp	24-Hour Festival	Nov.
Germany	Leverkusen	Opladen Beerex	Aug.
Netherlands	Amsterdam	Bokbierfestival	Oct./Nov.
Norway	Oslo	Bokkolfestival	Apr.
UK	London (usually)	Great British Beer Festival	Aug.
USA	Denver	Great American Beer Festival	Sept./Oct.

The Oktoberfest, held in Munich, Germany, during September/October, is by far the most internationally famous regional beer extravaganza.

INDEX OF BEERS

INDEX OF BEERS